User's Guide

to

ASTROLOGY

- Bruce Scofield -

One Reed Publications
1997

Published by *One Reed Publications*
PO Box 561, Amherst MA 01004-0561

ISBN 0-9628031-3-8

Editing and typesetting by Valerie Vaughan

Additional copies of this book may be ordered from the publisher. Please include $1.50 for postage and handling.

Chapter 4 is adapted from an article that first appeared in *American Astrology*, November, 1984.

Appendix B is a compilation of articles that appeared in *The Mountain Astrologer*, Mar.-May, 1994.

Horoscopes computed with *Solar Fire* software by Astrolabe.

Publisher's Cataloguing-in-Publication Data

Scofield, Bruce, 1948-
    User's guide to astrology / Bruce Scofield - 4th ed.
    144 p.
    Includes bibliographic references.
    Summary: Introductory guide to the history, theory, and practice of astrology, including specific techniques and exercises in astrological prediction and birthchart analysis.
    ISBN 0-9628031-3-8 (pbk.)
    1. Astrology--manuals. 2. Astronomy, Ancient. I. Title.
    133.5---dc20

Fourth Edition
First Printing 1997

Foreword

At the present time, astrology holds a very low status in the dominant culture. Writers and editors of magazines generally ignore the subject and studiously avoid using the "A" word, even when what they are discussing is clearly astrology. Television executives rarely allow the subject to be televised, and then only as entertainment. Scientists attack the subject at regular intervals, using the same old arguments. Intelligent responses from astrologers are suppressed. Colleges won't allow the subject to be taught, and any professors who show the slightest interest in it are ostracized, if not fired. Scientific studies that clearly show proof for astrology's claims are pushed under the rug. Only on Wall Street, where greed is king, does astrology get a hearing, and then only because it is perceived as an asset in the rush to material riches. In short, astrology is a banned subject, an underground study. On the surface it appears to have little or no influence on the cultural mainstream.

The reason why the dominant culture has rejected astrology is the same reason that is behind the 350-year effort to eliminate Native American cultures and their ecological approach to nature. It is the same reason why alternative medicine and natural healing have been ignored or attacked. The same reason explains the "conservative" backlash against the deeper messages of environmentalism.

Put simply, the fundamental assumptions that drive Western culture won't admit a subject that links man with nature. Western religions tell us that humanity is separate from nature, and nature is not to be trusted. Nature is bad. The high priests of modern science, in the service of politicians and corporations, promote an official agenda that ultimately supports a righteous dominance of man over nature. The scientists' unquestioned assumption, the same as in Western religion, is that nature is there to be conquered, manipulated, and exploited.

Astrology is rejected because it offers an alternative -- a deeper view into the workings of nature and the mysteries of existence. It offers a view that is inclusive, cosmic in scope, humbling, inspiring, and a challenge to some of our deepest assumptions about what is really going on in our lives. Astrology is a road map for living and a power tool for expanding awareness. Use it intelligently.

> *Ienciasca isa igba atfa acredsa owca.*
> -- Antipodes Astrologicon

Table of Contents

1. Astrology for Open Minds ...7

Astrology: Science or Art...7   Scientific Research on Astrology...9
Astrology and the Scientific Community...11   Common Objections to Astrology...12
The Two Zodiacs...12   Twins, Fate, & Free-Will...14
A Mechanism for Astrology...16   Astrology and Religion....18

2. What an Astrologer Does ...20

Many Types of Astrology...20   Calculating the Horoscope...21
Interpreting the Horoscope...22   Forecasting with Astrology...22
The Philosophy of an Astrologer...24   What Makes a Good Astrologer...24

3. The History of Astrology to 1500 ...26

Ancient Mesopotamia...27   India, China, and Mesoamerica...27
Ancient Greece...28   Ancient Rome...28   After the Fall of Rome...29

4. Why Did Astrology Decline? ...30

The Reformation...30   Loss of Royal Patronage...31
The Split Between Astrology and Astronomy...32   Rise of Modern Science...34
Other Factors in the Decline...35   Astrology Today...36

5. Planets and Other Points ...37

The Astronomy of the Solar System...38   Sun and Moon...39   Mercury, Venus, Mars...41
Psychological Model for the Inner Planets...42   The Asteroids...43   Jupiter and Saturn...44
Chiron: A Transitional Object...45   Uranus, Neptune, Pluto...46
The Planets as Symbols: Keywords and Concepts...49   The Ephemeris...51
Lunar and Planetary Nodes...52   The Part of Fortune...52   Hypothetical Planets...52
The Fixed Stars..:53

6. Aspects and Alignments ...54

The Principal Aspects: Harmonics 1 through 12...55   Parallel and Contraparallel...57
Hard vs. Soft Aspects...57   Major vs. Minor Aspects...58
Applying, Separating, and Orbs...58   A Summary of the Aspects...59   Midpoints...60

7. Signs of the Zodiac ...61

Why Twelve Signs?...61   The Zodiac and the Seasons...62
The Quadruplicities / Qualities...63   The Triplicities / Elements...64   The Polarities...64
The Signs Through the Year...64   Affinities With Planets...65   Sign Descriptions...66 ...
Aries...66   Taurus...67   Gemini...67   Cancer...68   Leo...69   Virgo...70   57
Hard vs. SoScorpio...71   Sagittarius...72   Capricorn...73   Aquarius...74   Pisces...75

8. Houses: Sectors of Sky ...76

The Ascendant & Midheaven Axes...77   House Systems...78   What the Houses Show...79
Meanings of the Houses...80   A Personal Zodiac...81   The Planets in the Houses...82
The Horoscope...84   Relocating the Houses: Astro-Mapping...85

9. Reading a Birth Chart ...86

Steps in Evaluating a Chart...86   Angular Planets...86   Elements and Qualities...86
Hemisphere Emphasis...88   An Astrological Personality Profile...89
Astrology & Self-Knowledge...91   Fate and Free-Will...93   Astrology & Mythology...93
Relationships...94   Synastry, the Composite Chart, and the Relationship Chart...95

10. Choosing the Best Time to Take Action ...97

The Phases of the Moon...97   Using Lunar Aspects...98   The Void-of-Course Moon...98
The Angularity of Sun, Jupiter, and Venus...98   Mercury Retrograde...100

11. Predicting with Transits ...101

Learning About Transits: An Exercise...103   The Transits of the Planets...104
The Seven-Year Cycle...108   The Graphic Ephemeris...108   Symbolic Substitution...110
Other Astrological Predictive Techniques...110

12. Doing Astrology on a Computer ...112

Low-End Introductory Software...114
High-End Delineation Packages and Report Writers...114
High-End Calculation Packages...115   Research Programs...116
Professional Interactive Programs...116   Specialized Astrology Programs...117
Miscellaneous Software...118   Where to Buy Astrological Software...119

Appendix A: *The Astrological Reading* ...120

Appendix B: *Calculating a Horoscope* ...124

Constructing a Chart with a Calculator...124   Chart Calculation Resources...133

Appendix C: *Tables of Planetary Positions* ...134

Mercury Stations...134   Venus Stations...135   Mars Ingresses...135
Jupiter Ingresses...136   Saturn Ingresses...136

Appendix D: *Astrological Publications and Resources* ...137

Books Recommended for Further Reading...136
Useful and Informative Periodicals...140   Sources for Astrological Software...140
National Astrological Organizations...141   Astrological Certifications...142
Astrological Chart Calculation Services...143   Directories of Practicing Astrologers...143

Preface

Today, there are books about astrology covering every aspect of the subject, including its history, practice, and philosophical implications. For those who want to learn something about the subject without investing in a lot of books, this guidebook is a good start. There are also people who have no intention of becoming astrologers, but merely want to be informed on the subject and need a handy general reference on astrology. Such people may read sections of this book, and then periodically refer to it when questions arise. Readers with a scientific background may find this book's practical information useful, as well as the section on the history of astrology and the arguments raised against it. In Part Three there are exercises in astrological prediction and a simple technique for analyzing a birth chart. This material is pragmatic, and may appeal to those with experimental inclinations. As the title suggests, the purpose of *User's Guide to Astrology* is to guide one through the full range of the subject. It does not pretend to be an exhaustive account, just a practical outline. The suggested readings in Appendix D will direct interested readers toward more complex and specialized works.

This guide began in 1981 as a twelve-page booklet entitled *Some Facts about Astrology*. In 1984, I expanded it to forty pages, adding hand-out material I had been using in classes and lectures. Then I re-titled it *Astrology for Open Minds* and printed several hundred copies. In 1987, I expanded the text to one hundred pages, keeping the same basic format, and changed the name to *User's Guide to Astrology*. In 1988, Pat White, Bill Sweeney, and Gary Christen of *Astrolabe, Inc.*, began to look over the manuscript, do some editing, and suggest additions and changes. I thank them for their input, particularly Gary and Bill for their substantial contributions to Chapter 12. I also wish to thank Valerie Vaughan, who proof-read and edited the manuscript several times. This latest incarnation, what seems to be a book with a life of its own, continues the format of factual, non-ideological astrology established back in 1981.

Chapter 1

Astrology for Open Minds

Dictionaries define astrology as a study that attempts to understand the affairs of human beings by studying the stars and planets. In essence, astrology is exactly that -- but it is also more. Astrologers read character and destiny from a map of the sky computed for the time and place of birth, a map called the horoscope. The positions of the planets in the horoscope symbolize a person's basic character, prominent personality traits, and also the timing of major life events. A good astrologer is even able to deduce something about a person's spouse, parents, children, and even pets from their horoscope. According to the prevailing belief systems of modern Western society, this should be impossible. A vast gulf separates those who embrace and practice astrology and those who do not. Before we get into the nuts and bolts of astrology itself, let's examine the controversial issues that surround the subject and try to answer the central question - "Is astrology real or fake?"

Astrology: Science or Art?

In the minds of skeptics, astrology is a *pseudo-science*, a subject that pretends to be a science. If this label means that there is no scientific foundation whatsoever for astrology, then the skeptics are either un-informed or hoodwinked by a cover-up that will be explained further on. If pseudo-science means that astrology does not entirely follow strict scientific methodologies, then the same accusation could be made against medicine or psychology. Both of these fields use a combination of scientific method (or technology) and personal judge-ment calls. We all know that some doctors are simply better than others. If the individual human element were taken out of medicine and all doctors and psychologists followed a strict set of scientific rules, we'd all be the worse for it. If the skeptic's standards for scientific worthiness were truly applied to the practice of medicine and psychology, these subjects would probably join astrology in the rejection bin. Apparently the skeptics don't know what they are talking about, so we must ask what exactly is astrology and how does it differ from accepted scientific studies like medicine and psychology?

A real understanding of astrology begins with the concept that it is basically a system, code, or language that uses symbols: the Sun, Moon and planets, zodiac signs, houses, and aspects. These symbols correspond to very specific categories of things, events, and personality traits. An astrologer blends combinations of these symbols and makes deductions about a person or situation. This act of interpretation is more like an art than a science. The only thing strictly scientific about astrology is the astronomy that is needed to create the schematic map of the sky commonly called the horoscope. Astrologers use astronomical data, mathematics, and computers to determine precisely how the sky was or will be configured at a given place and time. The rest of the work is basically intelligent interpretation of data. A close parallel to this kind of process would be a doctor's diagnosis of illness after a careful reading of several scientific tests and laboratory data.

Astrology differs from modern science because it uses a different kind of logic, one that assumes that things are interconnected. Science is obsessed with separations and boundaries that can be measured exactly. Astrology is holistic and works with connections and linkages. Science seeks control over nature while astrology seeks to work *with* nature. In a very real sense, astrology is concerned with interconnectedness -- the ecology of body, mind and spirit on this planet.

Astrology is sometimes attacked because much of it seems archaic to those trained in sciences that originated less than 200 years ago. The signs of the zodiac still retain their ancient names, and concepts like planetary rulership and house position are still a major part of the subject. It has retained connections to an earlier time when Man was not separate from Nature. The idea of the inter-connectedness of life, the earth, and the surrounding cosmic environment is similar to ideas held today in both the New Age and Environmentalist movements. Modern astrology is based on more than 4,000 years of observations that have been continually challenged and updated. Just as ancient medicine is not the medicine practiced today, ancient Mesopotamian or Renaissance astrology is not the astrology of the 20th century.

To understand astrology, it is important to keep in mind that it is very different from the "hard" sciences like physics or chemistry. Astrology can be a study in itself, like mathematics, but it is more often a practice like psychology and medicine, where scientific methodologies are applied to the human condition. Like psychology and medicine, astrology should be understood as a diagnostic art that uses scientific data.

Scientific Research on Astrology

Astrology hypothesizes that there is some form of correlation between the positions of celestial objects and the biological and meteorological processes on earth. In support of this hypothesis, there exists today a modest body of scientific research, most of it statistical. Partly because of a prejudice against astrology, the history of which is described in Chapters 3 and 4, funding for astrological research has not been forthcoming, and progress in finding supportive scientific evidence has been slow. For the time being, astrologers and supporters of astrology can cite only a few studies that clearly demonstrate that at least some parts of astrology are real and measurable. The most famous of these studies are those done by the French statisticians Michel Gauquelin and Francoise Schneider-Gauquelin.

Beginning in the mid-1950s and continuing through the 1980s, the Gauquelins published a number of books and reports on their statistical studies of astrology. Their research centered on the effects of planets on profession, personality traits, and heredity. Since ancient times, astrologers have claimed that the location of a planet at the time of a person's birth indicates its relative ability to affect that individual's personality and life. The Gauquelins began their study by first accumulating birth data on thousands of persons and then determining where each planet was located relative to the horizon at the time and place of birth. For example, for a person born at noon, the Sun would be in the middle of the sky overhead; at dusk, on the western horizon. The same kind of analysis was done for the Moon, Mercury, Venus, Mars, Jupiter, and Saturn.

In one study, done in 1955, Michel Gauquelin plotted the position of Mars relative to the horizon for a sample of 2,000 sports champions. (According to astrology, Mars is associated symbolically with sports.) If there were no planetary effect, one would expect Mars to be randomly distributed in the sample. Instead, the study showed that Mars was situated more often in the sectors located just after rising, setting, upper culmination, and lower culmination. A control group of people who were not sports champions showed an even distribution of Mars through the sky. The Gauquelins found similar correlations for Saturn in the birthcharts of scientists, Jupiter with famous actors, Venus with writers, and the Moon with writers and politicians.

9

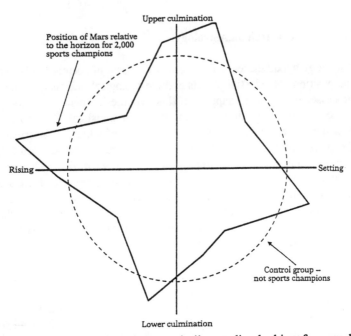

Upper culmination

Position of Mars relative
to the horizon for 2,000
sports champions

Rising

Setting

Control group –
not sports champions

Lower culmination

The Gauquelins conducted many similar studies looking for correlations between known facts about a group of people and the location of a particular planet at the time of birth. They also found what appears to be evidence of a kind of planetary heredity: a planet located in one of the emphasized sectors of the sky tended to be duplicated in the birthcharts of offspring. In later studies by the Gauquelins, personality traits showed an even clearer correlation than profession did. These studies suggested that the real link with the planets is with personality, not profession, which is usually a choice dictated by personality.

The Gauquelin work shows that certain astrological principles can be demonstrated through rather complex and time-consuming statistical studies. Other tenets of astrology are more difficult to test because of the individual nature of each horoscope and the different interpretation styles used by experienced astrologers. Statistical testing in the field of psychology is similarly difficult and controversial due to the complex nature of human personality. The big difference between psychological and astrological scientific studies is that the former gets plenty of funding, the later is done by independent researchers who bear the costs themselves. Because research can be extremely complex, time-consuming, and costly, much astrology remains to be tested.

Astrology and the Scientific Community

The Gauquelin findings were successfully replicated many times, both by themselves and by independent statisticians. Nevertheless, their work has so far made little impact on the scientific community. To give you some idea of the limitations imposed on astrology and astrologers by skeptical scientists, here is the story of the their reaction to the Gauquelin studies.

In 1975, the *Humanist* magazine dedicated the 100th anniversary of the American Ethical Union to the discrediting of astrology. On the very first pages of the September/October issue was a list of 186 scientists, including 18 Nobel prize winners, who had signed a statement saying that astrology was essentially superstition and that there was no verifiable scientific basis for a belief in it. The rest of the issue included a number of anti-astrology articles.

One of the articles in the *Humanist* attacked the methodology of the Gauquelin's astrological experiments. Michel Gauquelin responded by challenging the skeptics to replicate the experiments. The Committee for the Scientific Investigation of the Claims of the Paranormal (CSICOP), a kind of self-appointed scientific thought-police, agreed to do this. They soon made public their conclusions - that Gauquelin's claims were false and astrology was again pronounced dead. This announcement was loudly broadcasted. For several years, numerous articles and stories appeared in magazines and newspapers reporting that the scientists were absolutely correct about Gauquelin's statistical studies being faulty. But also during this period, one of the original CSICOP skeptics resigned and published evidence (in *Fate* magazine, October 1981) that the CSICOP replications of Gauquelin's experiments actually agreed with his conclusions, and that this fact had been covered up. Gauquelin, realizing that he was dealing with a situation that was far from scientific, pressed on and was eventually vindicated after several independently conducted studies checked and confirmed the correctness of his work. Soon after, some scientists submitted a tiny notice to the *Skeptical Inquirer* (Spring 1983), reporting that Gauquelin's studies had withstood their challenge. But most of the general public, which had heard all the negative attacks on astrology, never heard the eventual outcome of this debate.

Historians of science have long observed that so-called "scientific truths" can change over time. What was believed to be true 100 years ago may now be considered false. What was false 100 years ago may now be considered truth. Science, like all human endeavors, is strongly affected by dominant personalities who have reasons for keeping things a certain way. While scientific methods may point to the need for a change in thinking, historians know that a scientific revolution will only occur when the supporters of the older view die or retire. Good examples of this can be found in the resistance that established scientists have had, and still have, to supposedly radical concepts like homeopathy and acupuncture (alternative medicine), extraterrestrial intelligence, and even intelligence in the higher primates (gorillas, chimpanzees, and orangutans). Strong evidence is never enough for these obstructors of progress who use the banner of science to preserve their respectability. As usual, dominant personalities will have it their way. We are dealing with something like this in regard to the Gauquelin tests of astrology.

Today, the main attackers of astrology are skeptical scientists and clergymen, and in nearly every case these people know next to nothing about the subject. Maintaining that their definition of reality is demonstrably the only one, they use their positions of authority to silence their critics. For centuries they have used the same arguments against astrology. Though they have not succeeded in eliminating astrology, they have been successful in keeping it out of the intellectual mainstream, and consequently out of funding, for the past three hundred years. Let's now take a look at these perennial arguments.

Common Objections to Astrology

The most common objections raised by the scientific critics of astrology are: the problem of the two zodiacs, the question of the destinies of twins, fate vs. free-will, and the lack of a scientific explanation for how astrology works. Let's look at these issues more closely.

The Two Zodiacs

The best-known part of astrology today is the zodiac, a 12-fold division of the path that the Sun and planets follow in their movements through the sky. The zodiacal sign in which the Sun was positioned at a person's birth has come to be known as his or her "sign." For many people, this is all the astrology they are ever exposed to. Newspapers and magazines, in their efforts to interest as many people as possible, devote regular columns to this sort of astrological interpretation. In the history of astrology, these Sun-sign "horoscopes," which promote a simplistic view of the subject, are a relatively recent phenomena.

Most Western astrologers use the *tropical zodiac* which is tied to the cycle of the seasons. The beginning of this zodiac is the point where the Sun is on the first day of spring in the Northern Hemisphere. Astronomers use a *sidereal zodiac*, as do astrologers in India and some Western astrologers. This zodiac is tied to the relatively unchanging positions of the stars and constellations. About 2,000 years ago, these two types of zodiacs coincided. Since that time, a slow movement of the earth's axis has caused the two types of zodiacs to separate by about 26 degrees. This westward movement of the vernal point (where the Sun is on the first day of spring) through the constellations is known as the *precession of the equinoxes*. It is this movement which gives rise to the notion of the astrological "ages." According to many astrologers, we are presently near the end of the age of Pisces and approaching the age of Aquarius, due to begin in a century or so.

The tropical zodiac divides the year into twelfths, with key points at the beginning of the seasons. Each twelfth occupies 30 degrees of the Sun's path through the sky as seen from the earth. These 12 divisions are the familiar zodiac signs which are said to modify the influence of the Sun, Moon, and any planet located within them. The tropical zodiac has nothing to do with the constellations made up of stars, though it does have something to do with the seasons and the fact that we have 12 months in our year.

The sidereal zodiac used by astronomers is a division of the year based on the location of the Sun in the groups of stars called the constellations. Since the constellations are not all of equal size, the time that the Sun spends in a sign varies. The names of these zones on the Sun's path are taken from the constellations located there. Technically, there are actually 13 constellations that intercept the Sun's path; the familiar 12 constellations of the zodiac plus the constellation Ophiuchus, located between Scorpio and Sagittarius. Periodically, astronomers intent on debunking astrology will announce to the media that astrologers haven't noticed that there is a 13th sign. Because the media and the public are so poorly informed about astrology, they haven't noticed that these astronomers are really grinding an axe and are quite ignorant of astrology. Zodiacs are spatial frameworks created to measure the position of an astronomical body. If a birthchart or horoscope could be compared to a meal set on a table, a change of zodiacs would be comparable to a change of tablecloths. Both the dinner spread and the table itself would remain in the same place relative to each other, though the backdrop would be different.

13

The influence of the tropical zodiac, which has traditionally been said to modify the basic nature of the Sun, Moon, and planets, has not yet been conclusively proven through statistical analysis. Separating the influences of the Sun, Moon, and planets in order to measure them presents serious problems for the researcher. However, several studies done by astrologer Jeff Mayo and psychologist Hans J. Eysenck have shown that the zodiacal position of the Sun appear to correlate with introversion and extroversion in personality. Their work seems to confirm the traditional astrological notion that the fire and air signs tend to be extroverted while the water and earth signs are introverted. While these studies are certainly important, many principles of astrology stand independent of any zodiac. It is unfortunate that the public has come to associate the entire field of astrology with the tropical zodiac, and to believe that the subject should either stand or fall according to the validity of zodiacal Sun-signs. In fact, certain schools of astrology, notably Cosmobiology and the Hamburg School founded by Alfred Witte, are able to give complete readings of horoscopes without any reference to zodiacal signs.

Twins, Fate, and Free-Will

Another common argument brought against astrology concerns twins. Critics ask, how can twins be different if they were born at the same place and at nearly the same time? Interestingly, the astrologer's answer to this question gives insight into the fate versus free-will problem, a stumbling block for many trying to evaluate astrology and a common point of attack by clergymen.

There is much evidence that twins separated at birth very often follow a strikingly similar path. There are many dramatic reports, past and present, of separated twins leading almost exactly parallel lives. The University of Minnesota has long researched twins and has noted this strange phenomenon. Of course, scientists attribute these similarities to genetics; ignoring astrological configurations in the birthchart. While twins raised apart show similarities, twins who are raised together are often quite dissimilar in personality and life progress. These differences may be evidence of free-will. Astrologers suggest that separated twins follow similar life patterns, ones imprinted at birth and symbolized in the birthchart, and that they do this quite naturally because their individual identities are not threatened by being in constant contact and competition with each other. Astrologers note that twins will typically choose different parts of their birthcharts around which to build an identity.

For example, consider twins born when the Sun was in Gemini and the Moon was in Taurus. One twin might focus primarily on Gemini and build his identity around that sign's characteristics. The other twin would then construct his identity around the motivations and themes symbolized by Taurus.

Twins raised together often exhibit synchronicity in their life patterns on a very basic level. For example, an astrologer might forecast that both twins would have a relationship crisis at a certain time. At the designated time, one twin marries and the other separates from a relationship. Is this a case of astrological failure? The astrologer would argue it wasn't by pointing out that both twins had to confront relationship issues at the designated time. The fact that each chose a different path is further proof of free-will. While astrology suggests that we follow a precise timetable symbolized by the distribution of the planets at the time and place of our birth, it also shows that we can make our own decisions and exert our own will if we choose. For astrologers, twins illustrate the fact that we have freedom of choice, if we want it.

One of the assumptions usually made in regard to twin births is that they both have the same horoscope. From a broad astrological perspective, that is true, and that is what accounts for the similarities between twins. However, technical experts in astrology would argue that a separation of even one minute of time between the births can account for some significant differences. For example, one twin could be born with the last degree of Aries rising, and the other, born only one minute later, could have the first degree of Taurus rising. While the arc separating the births is small, the sign difference is great, and this would signify very different identities.

Astrologers would also point out that a difference of four minutes between births can account for a year's difference in the timing of a major life event. One twin might experience a certain kind of stress at a developmentally vulnerable time. The other could experience the stress a year later and consequently have a very different experience. There are other techniques in astrology, including midpoint analysis and harmonic charts, that reveal significant differences between horoscopes separated by very small amounts of time.

A Mechanism for Astrology

The question scientists most often ask in regard to astrology is -- How does it work? The current answer is that no one really knows how it works, but astrologers have learned how to work with it. This is not so different from the commonplace yet barely understood phenomenon called electricity. Practical use was being made of electricity long before a modern understanding of it was attained, and such an understanding is still far from complete. Another example is the less common, though well-funded, world of particle physics. In this arcane area of research, mysterious particles (that are also waves) are identified, but not truly understood. In chemistry, the exact nature of the effect aspirin has on a feverish body is also in this category. While something is known about it now, for many years it was a complete mystery -- yet people got benefits from aspirin. Perhaps the best way to deal with the question of a scientific explanation for how astrology works is to suggest that there may be an acceptable one in the future, but we are without one for the present.

A number of theories have been forwarded concerning the nature of the link between terrestrial life and the Sun, Moon, and planets. For many years, physical cause-and-effect theories of astrology have drawn attention to the gravitational effects of the Moon and its obvious links to tides and biological cycles. Serious studies, as well as the personal experiences of nurses and policemen, do seem to show a link between the phases of the Moon and crime rates, hemorrhaging, and other sorts of crises. While the Moon, and to a much lesser extent, the Sun, exert a measurable gravitational effect on the earth, that of the other planets is extremely small. Scientists like to say the gravitational effect of the obstetrician to a newborn is greater than that of the planets. Since all the planets are used in astrology, perhaps gravity is only a partial explanation for the astrological effect.

Other physical theories have been forwarded to explain how planets could affect a person. John Nelson, a radio-storm forecaster for RCA, found that specific angular separations between the planets coincided with solar disturbances and consequent magnetic field disruptions on the earth. It is true that man and other life forms have electromagnetic fields; perhaps life on earth is affected by these subtle changes in the earth's magnetic field. It is apparent to many astrologers that planets moving slowly seem to have a greater effect than those moving rapidly. Pluto, which moves very slowly from the perspective of the earth, seems to have an extremely potent astrological effect. Mercury normally moves very quickly, but when it reaches a part of its orbit relative to the earth where it appears to slow down, its effects become stronger. It may be that the longer a planet occupies a specific position, the stronger is its effect on the magnetic field of the earth, or perhaps the human body itself. It has been argued that amniotic fluid shields the magnetic field to some degree and that only at birth is the brain exposed, and imprinted, with the field's pattern at that moment.

Other theories suggest that a preoccupation with a physical cause-and-effect linkage may be misleading and that perhaps the nature of life is far more complex than most scientists suspect. Although most astrology books, including this one, focus primarily on the astrology of human life, this is only one of many applications that astrology has to offer. Any astrologer will tell you that charts made for events, such as the opening of a business, a marriage, or a launch, work perfectly. Charts calculated for the time that the Sun is exactly at the equinoxes or solstices are used for weather forecasting. These are charts for supposedly inanimate processes -- but how inanimate are they? By accepting the fact that astrology works, we are challenged to question assumptions about the way the world and human consciousness operates. Astrology opens up a vista into the nature of our existence that is mind-boggling, to say the least.

Some astrologers have found that psychologist Carl G. Jung's idea of synchronicity is appealing as an explanation. From this point of view the astrological effect is non-causal; humanity and the planets are only parts of a much larger cosmic psychic process. Jung used the idea of synchronicity to explain things like simultaneous discoveries and other strange coincidences. Two things happening at the same time (for example, an alignment of Mars and Venus and the arousal of passionate love) may not necessarily be directly connected, but may be indirectly unified because both are part of a larger picture.

Scientific metaphysical thinking has become more sophisticated in recent years. We've seen a number of books published that draw parallels between the strange world of particle physics and the occult philosophies of eastern religions, which in turn support astrology. Chaos theory, fractals, Rupert Sheldrake's theory of formative causation, and the theory of the holographic universe -- all these ideas open up vast perspectives against which astrology might be explained. But for the present, one can only say that much work needs to be done before this persistent question can be answered with certainty.

Astrology and Religion

People who are unfamiliar with astrology (including scientists) have sometimes regarded it as a religion. While it is true that the gods for which the planets were named were worshiped in ancient times, astrology itself has always been a study and a practical body of knowledge, not a ritual based on faith. The monotheistic religions of the Western world, in their quest for uniformity of belief, have long held an ambivalent relationship with astrology. They have, at different times, found it both useful and threatening, supportive and undermining. In general, though, organized Western religions have kept a safe distance from astrology. The more tolerant religions of the East have not had such a problematic relationship with the subject, and some have even incorporated astrology into their programs for spiritual enlightenment.

In the Bible, astrology is represented in both positive and negative ways. In *Genesis,* God creates the Sun and Moon as signs in the sky, as well to determine the seasons, days, and years. In *Matthew* (2), it is the astrologers (*magi*) who are first on the scene in recognizing the importance of the birth of Christ. They also hear the word of God and refuse to cooperate with Herod.

Religious leaders who attack astrology usually use biblical quotations out of context to support their arguments. For example, in *Isaiah* (47) and *Daniel* (2-5), it is the astrologers of the ancient Near East, not astrology itself, that are attacked as being incompetent, misguided, and inferior to Daniel, God's master dream-interpreter and psychic.

Religious skeptics generally fail to make any distinctions between astrology and practices such as witchcraft, fortune-telling, serpent charming, or necromancy. This is unfortunate and only continues a long tradition of ignorance and misunderstanding of the true nature of the subject. There is nothing in astrology that repudiates religion, and most astrologers have strong spiritual inclinations. It could be said, however, that knowledge of astrology leads one to a view of life that is not exclusive to one religion, but inclusive of many alternative forms of spirituality.

Conclusion

Hopefully, this brief outline will help to compensate for the lack of factual information available to the public. Newspaper horoscopes and 900 telephone lines are assumed by many to be all that astrology has to offer. But Sun-sign horoscope columns are about as representative of astrology as the Dear Abby advice columns are of psychology. Most people are prejudiced against astrology because they have been programmed by the media to view it as entertainment. It never occurs to them that there is a vast body of serious writing and research on the subject available in libraries and bookstores. Certain popular science writers scoff at astrology but make no effort to inform themselves as to its subtleties. When those who have the podium (i.e. the scientists, academicians, politicians, and clergy) reject astrology out of hand, the average person, who is prone to let others do his thinking for him, is apt to do the same.

With few exceptions, those who regard astrology as superstition or self-deception know virtually nothing about it. Because astrology has not been fashionable, these people are not embarrassed by their prejudice. In fact, the chief reason most people resist astrology is because its acceptance is not already commonplace or politically correct. As we approach the next century all this seems to be changing.

Chapter 2:

What an Astrologer Does

Today the most widely practiced branch of astrology is natal astrology (historically known as genethliacal astrology), which concerns itself with the character and destiny of individuals. From the positions of the Sun, Moon, and planets at the time and place of birth, the practitioner of natal astrology attempts to analyze the basic nature and predisposition of an individual, and to forecast future life trends. It is this branch of astrology that is the primary concern of this book. It should be mentioned that there are several other important branches of astrology besides natal. These are widely practiced yet have a lower public profile.

Many Types of Astrology

Mundane astrology concerns itself with historical and political trends. This includes predictions of changes in government, election forecasts, wars, or the astrological analysis of a nation's history. Mundane astrology was the earliest known type of astrology, practiced at least 4,000 years ago by astrologers in ancient Mesopotamia.

Astrometeorology is the study of correlations between planetary configurations and the weather. This branch also dates back to the origins of astrology and is still practiced today. The weather forecasts in popular almanacs were, and often still are today, based on astrometeorology. There is now scientific research that supports some astrometeorological principles (for example, see *Science* (1962), Vol. 137, pp. 748-750).

Horary astrology, which means the "astrology of the hour," is a technique that is used to answer questions with a chart cast for the time the question was asked. This branch of astrology, which does not require an exact birth time, was widely practiced during the Roman Empire and the Renaissance. It is still used by many of today's practitioners of natal astrology.

Electional astrology is concerned with computing in advance the best time to take important actions such as opening a business or getting married. In the past, merchants relied greatly on this technique, and ships were launched for the first time, or set sail for distant ports, at precise times set by astrologers.

Medical astrology is concerned with the analysis of disease through astrological symbolism. It was practiced by Hippocrates, Galen, Culpepper, and many other physicians throughout history. One common technique used by medical astrologers of the past was to calculate a horoscope for the time that the patient became ill and took to bed, or was injured. An analysis of such a chart gave the practitioner insights into what might be the best treatment for the patient. In earlier times, medical practitioners frequently relied on herbs for cures. Each herb was linked to a specific astrological symbol.

Calculating the Horoscope

No matter what type of astrology is being practiced, all astrologers base their interpretations on the positions of the Sun, Moon, and planets. As in other fields of study, individual practitioners vary in the techniques they use. Some astrologers include the positions of certain asteroids, some add hypothetical bodies, some use stars, quasars, and even the galactic center. All these positions are calculated from precise astronomical tables for the exact time and place of an event or a person's birth. The resulting information is usually noted on a circular chart which has come to be known as the horoscope. More detailed astronomical information that is derived from the horoscope is often listed on separate pages.

The position of the Sun, Moon, or a planet at the time of birth is a constant, and all astrologers must deal with this position as it is. Only a miscalculation accounts for any real differences in chart construction. There can, however, be minor differences which are due to variations in method, such as the following. Although most astrologers today use the tropical zodiac (mentioned in Chapter 1), some (including Hindu astrologers) use the sidereal zodiac. While this does not alter the relationships between the planets and the horizon, it often changes the sign that they are located in. Practicing astrologers must also choose which house system they will use in their work. (The house systems are methods of dividing the sky and are discussed in Chapter 8.) There is no universally agreed-upon house system, and sometimes a planet's house position in one system will change in another system. Procedural differences such as these are also common in other disciples, notably psychology and medicine.

Today, most professional astrologers use computers, which free them from laborious but necessary mathematical calculations. One benefit of computers is that they allow astrologers to experiment with a variety of techniques. In time, it is possible that a consensus may arise as to which ones work more consistently.

Interpreting the Horoscope

The real difference among astrologers lies in the way the data is interpreted. As in other interpretive fields like medicine and psychology, it is the practitioner's individual skills that count most. In interpreting a birthchart, the astrologer uses the planets as a set of symbols that are uniquely arranged at every birth. Each planet is said to symbolize a specific psychological urge. For example, Mars is said to symbolize assertiveness. If Mars were rising at the time and place of a birth, most astrologers would agree that the assertive qualities of that individual would be prominent, resulting most often in a bold, competitive, and possibly combative personality.

To the competent astrologer, interpreting astrological symbols in a birthchart can reveal many things: an individual's early life experiences, inherited predispositions, and basic life challenges. Essentially, the astrologer seeks to understand a person's potential, and in a positive sense, can often bring into focus hidden strengths and talents. The astrologer offers to individuals an account of who they are, where they have been, and where they might go in order to realize their potential. Unlike the psychologist, the astrologer can reach such conclusions rapidly, even without ever having met the client.

The technical skills of horoscope interpretation do not necessarily guarantee that the practitioner will have "a way with people." The best practicing astrologers are also skilled counselors and consultants with extensive experience and a solid knowledge of human nature. They must be able to use computers and handle mathematical problems, understand psychological terminology and theory, and be able to counsel people who may be going through difficult times in their lives. These are not ordinary qualifications, and being a practicing astrologer is no easy job.

Forecasting with Astrology

Probably the most controversial, intriguing, and popular aspect of astrology has to do with the prediction of the future. Strictly speaking, predicting an exact event in the future is impossible. What the astrologer can do is forecast the nature of trends and locate points in time when physical, social, or psychological events may occur. Astrologers find that, while the *timing* of an event or trend is reliably predictable, a person's *response* to the event is not. While the timing of specific circumstances appears to be fated (or pre-programmed), our free-will can color the nature and quality of our responses.

There is nothing inherently mystical in astrological forecasting, as you will see in the following example. The first necessity is an ephemeris, or book of tables, which contains the positions of the planets for each day. Using these tables (or a computer), the astrologer is able to compute charts showing the positions of the Sun, Moon, and planets in relation to a specific time and place on Earth.

As an example, let us use the birthchart of former President Richard Nixon. At the time of his birth, the Sun was at 19 degrees of Capricorn. This means that for his entire life, Richard Nixon was sensitive to this degree area. The position of the Sun in a birthchart symbolizes a person's physical body, vitality, and personal power, and the sign Capricorn symbolizes profession, honor, and reputation. As you might well imagine, the Sun in Capricorn would be a very important point in the birthchart of this president. In late 1974, the planet Saturn, symbolizing obstacles and problems, was transiting (moving) through the 19th degree of Cancer, exactly opposite the sign and degree of the Sun at Nixon's birth. Astrologers call this alignment "transiting Saturn in opposition to the natal Sun." The transit itself is an "absolute" astrological fact, but it is abstract and without meaning until the astrologer calls upon his knowledge of astrological symbolism to make sense of this alignment and offer an interpretation.

Transiting Saturn being opposite Nixon's Sun degree in late 1974 suggests that he would encounter obstacles at this time. The accumulated experiences of thousands of astrologers over the past 2,500 years has shown that the opposition of Saturn to the Sun often occurs around the time of an important life decision, made under pressure. It has also been observed that problems tend to accumulate in a person's life at such a time, and frequently a decision is made to separate from something, often a residence, a job, or a marriage. Not every case is the same, but there is a general pattern recognized by astrologers today and historically.

Now, since we know that Nixon's Sun position symbolizes his honor and status, and that Saturn opposite the Sun often symbolizes problems and possible separations, we could make a prediction. We could state that, "in the latter part of 1974, Richard Nixon will face a great challenge to his status and may choose to pull back or separate from his professional life." Interestingly, many astrologers made such a forecast prior to his resignation from the presidency in August, 1974. There is more about astrological forecasting in Chapter 11.

The Philosophy of an Astrologer

While there is no universally accepted philosophy or belief system associated with astrology, one could say that most astrologers do see a unity in all things. Frequent confirmation of the idea that the planets have correlations with life on earth leads one toward expansive and inclusive philosophical positions. Astrologers see and experience the linkages in all of nature, and they attempt to work with nature, rather than to dominate or control it.

Many astrologers believe in some form of reincarnation, though there is nothing in astrology that makes this belief necessary. During the late 19th and early 20th centuries, a number of prominent astrologers were associated with the Theosophical Society, a group that embraces reincarnation. Many who learned from these astrologers have assumed a close linkage between the two. Reincarnation is, however, a belief that may be held by persons in any walk of life. It is not supported any more by astrology than it is by psychology.

What Makes a Good Astrologer?

Astrologers may be self-taught or study under a teacher, and after years of practice, emerge as respected professionals. Some astrologers learn and practice only one type of astrology, while others are more versatile. Unlike medicine and law, astrology today has no universally accepted standards. This situation is changing, however, since there are now astrological organizations that offer certification. One is the American Federation of Astrologers (AFA), which offers an 8-hour professional-level test, the passing of which guarantees that a person knows the mathematical side of astrology thoroughly and can also interpret a natal chart reasonably well. The National Council for Geocosmic Research (NCGR) offers a far more thorough and demanding certification program with four levels, from beginner to professional, with examinations at each level. These and other certifying astrological organizations are listed in Appendix D.

Merely passing a difficult test, however, is no guarantee that someone is competent. Some doctors and lawyers have passed licensing tests, yet they are still not fit to practice. Also, astrologers are capable of explaining through astrology only what they are capable of understanding. A good astrologer needs a knowledge of human nature. A degree in psychology or one of the other social sciences is useful in this regard. Ultimately the practice of astrology is interpretive and diagnostic, and proficiency comes with experience. Like the best doctors, the best astrologers are those who have perfected their judgment over a long period of time. For information on astrological readings and what you could expect from one, see Appendix A.

Chapter 3:

The History of Astrology to 1500

Since ancient times, agricultural communities have relied on a knowledge of the changes of the seasons and the fertility cycles of animals. Observing the movements of the Sun and Moon and their correlations with these crucial biological rhythms led to the development of the first science -- astrology, astronomy, and the calendar, which were essential for civilization and an orderly community life.

Early humans lived close to nature. They noticed that the point in the east at which the Sun rises every day changes throughout the year, and that this movement coincides with the changes of the seasons. They saw that the cycle of the Moon was linked to mammalian fertility cycles. They built calendar sites and temples aligned to the points on the horizon where these regular astronomical phenomena occurred. Pyramids and temples in Egypt and Mexico, as well as stone circles like Stonehenge in the British Isles, have survived from ancient times, testifying to the importance of skywatching in the development of civilization.

As civilization progressed, the phases of the Moon, eclipses, and the cycles of the planets were recorded and compared with events on earth. Floods, political changes, wars, economic fluctuations, and events in people's lives were correlated with activity in the sky. Over the years, certain relationships became apparent. These empirical correlations became the basis for the astrology practiced today. In ancient times, humankind was believed to be a part of, not separate from, nature. The linking of the movements of the Sun, Moon, and planets with human life was obvious to humanity worldwide. Eventually, astrology, astronomy, and calendar science developed as a single body of knowledge that studied humanity's relationship to the astronomical cycles.

Although religious significance was often attached to the planets and to particular days in the yearly cycle (as it still is today), astrology was not, in itself, a religion. It was a system of knowledge based on accumulated observations, and it gave early humanity some sense of security and order in an otherwise unpredictable world.

Ancient Mesopotamia

Relationships between humans and their celestial environment were noted throughout the world wherever civilization developed. But it was in ancient Mesopotamia, a region of acute instability, that this activity reached its zenith. Here, astronomical and atmospheric phenomena were observed, carefully recorded, and interpreted for the ruling elite by astronomer-priests. This may have begun with the Sumerians, perhaps the oldest civilization in the Near East, but it was sustained and developed by the Akkadians, Assyrians, Babylonians, and other civilizations that flourished in the region up to the age of the Romans. Detailed observations were made more or less continuously for several thousand years. Ultimately, astrology in Mesopotamia became a highly sophisticated omen system based on rigorous astronomical observations and the accumulated experience of generations of sky interpreters. It influenced religion, philosophy, government, and politics. Our seven-day week, each day of which is named for a planet, is an astrological remnant of ancient Near Eastern sky-consciousness.

India, China and Mesoamerica

Astrology also developed elsewhere. In India, an ancient native astrology blended with Greco-Mesopotamian astrology to produce a unique system still practiced today. Astrology has always been popular in India, and it has not suffered the discrediting it has experienced in most Western cultures. There are astrological colleges in India and the subject is employed at the highest levels of government.

In China, astrologers favored a polar-based system of measurement, in contrast to the Mesopotamian measuring system which was based on the Sun's path or ecliptic. The Chinese, as well as the Indians, also used something like a twenty-eight-sign zodiac, based on the motion of the Moon. The popular 12-year cycle of animals in Chinese astrology is only one part of a more complex system based around cycles of 12 and 10 that is still virtually unknown in the West.

At the time of the Spanish Conquest, Mesoamerica (Mexico and northern Central America) was as culturally advanced as ancient Mesopotamia, India, and China. It also had a form of astrology, a unique form that emphasized time. (In the West, sky events were measured spatially; in Mexico, time itself acted like a zodiacal sign.) The ancient Maya, Toltec, and Aztec astrologers used a sequence of 20 days that acted like zodiacal signs and which repeated endlessly, much like our 7-day week. These 20 day-signs cycled with 13 sacred numbers, producing an astrological calendar of 260 days. Other astronomical cycles, ranging from days to millennia, were part of this astrological system. The ancient Mesoamericans also held the planet Venus in high regard and made predictions based on its movements.

While the indigenous Hindu, Chinese, and Mesoamerican astrological systems were quite sophisticated and held potential for further development, the astrology practiced today throughout the Western world is rooted in the astrology of ancient Mesopotamia.

Ancient Greece

During the centuries before and after Alexander's conquest of the Near East, there was contact between Greece and Mesopotamia which led to significant developments in astrology. An emphasis on the geometrical properties of planetary relationships (the aspects) led to a more complex analysis of the sky. It was during this period that the 12-sign zodiac, which had been developing for hundreds of years, became a major feature. The Greek mind, which sought neatness and organization, arranged the various components of Mesopotamian astrology into a system structured by spatial geometry.

The notion of a map of the heavens calculated for the time and place of a person's birth (the horoscope) was probably the most important development during this period. Originally, Mesopotamian astrology had concerned itself mainly with the life of the nation or kingdom. The king was the center of the human world and only the planets at his birth were considered worth examining. But the oldest surviving horoscope (410 B.C.) was made for a commoner. The Greeks, who placed a high value on the individual, stimulated the transition in astrology from a study of the King and the kingdom to the study of individual lives.

Ancient Rome

When Rome became the dominant Mediterranean power, astrology gained in prestige and influence. Astrologers were often the most learned men of their times, and most emperors relied on their advice. At least two emperors, Tiberius and Hadrian, were practicing astrologers themselves. There were plenty of public practitioners as well. Astrology was supported by Stoicism, a philosophy popular with many leading Romans. At certain times, astrological predictions of the deaths of famous persons became so excessive that mass expulsions of astrologers were ordered and laws were passed to regulate the practice of astrology. During the Roman Empire, many books on astrology were written, several of which survive. The most famous, the *Tetrabiblos* of Claudius Ptolemy, was written around A.D. 150 and became the major handbook of astrology during the Middle Ages and Renaissance. The techniques of Roman astrologers were very sophisticated, and many are still used today or have served to stimulate new developments in the field.

Until recently, only a small portion of the many surviving Greek and Roman astrological writings were translated into English. Also, most translations were done by scholars hostile to astrology. To remedy this situation, *Project Hindsight*, was founded in 1992 to reclaim astrology's ancient roots. Funded entirely by the astrological community, several astrologically-minded translators have produced excellent translations of important and valuable ancient astrological writings. These have opened up some unique perspectives on the subject which are stimulating lively discussions within the field.

After the Fall of Rome

While Europe was in the Dark Ages, the Islamic world became the bright light of Western civilization. The scientific works of the Greeks and Romans had suffered at the hands of Christian fanatics, but in intellectual centers like Baghdad and in Moslem Spain they were copied and recopied. Arab scientists also made some significant advancement in the field. In order to avoid potential religious conflicts, Arabic astrology focused on historical and political astrology rather than on human births. During the 12th and 13th centuries, Arab manuscripts began to circulate in Europe. This influx of information brought about a revival of astrology, accompanied by Christian rationalizations for its existence by none other than the Church father, Thomas Aquinas. Within a few centuries astrology was being taught in the universities, and most Italian courts included an astrologer. By the 15th century, astrology had regained the social position it had held in the West for most of its earlier history. It was practiced by the most learned men, used by leaders for decision-making, and served as a model for understanding the cosmos and the meaning of life.

Up until the 16th and 17th centuries in the West, astrology and astronomy were usually practiced by the same person. After this, they became separated and astrology experienced another decline. The reasons for this are complex and will be examined in Chapter 4.

Chapter 4:

Why Did Astrology Decline?

In the middle of the High Renaissance, the early sixteenth century, astrology was being taught in the universities and practiced in the courts of kings. By the end of this century, its prestige had declined considerably. It could be said that the decline of astrology began in 1497 when Pico della Mirandola, the great humanist and religious fanatic, published his book *Disputes on Astrology*. Pico argued that astrology should be rejected because it denied free-will to humans and power to God. In his view, humans were self-contained beings having the power to improve themselves. "If this is so," he argued, "how can he [Man] be controlled by the planets?" Pico saw God as the ultimate power who would send angels to help men on special occasions. He argued that God certainly wouldn't use the planets as agents of His will, so the planets could also have no real effects on Man in this sense. In his attack on astrology, Pico selected information that supported his arguments but he suppressed any to the contrary. Pico could have been accused of twisting the facts, but to those who knew nothing about astrology, he seemed to be speaking the truth with intense passion and great authority.

Pico's attack on astrology had all the conviction and supreme confidence of a religious fanatic. But even more important for our concern is the fact that his book became an encyclopedia of arguments against astrology that were used by other objectors. Many other works were written against astrology over the next two hundred years, and much of the material was taken directly from Pico. Most of these attacks on astrology were for religious reasons.

The Reformation

From about 1520 onwards, religious passions were aroused all over Europe which led to educational, political, and economic changes. Religious wars and conflicts drew everyone's attention. Religious reforms, initiated by powerful men like Luther and Calvin, emphasized the importance of the individual and his relationship to God, not the planets or stars. In a world of uncertainty, death, and famine, people sought explanations which both astrologer and priest were able to provide. Religious leaders therefore saw astrology as serious competition. For the next 150 years, the clergy attacked astrology with a vengeance. Overall, the astrologers were more flexible and inclusive. They could believe in God, be Christians, and still practice their art, which they argued was created by God in the first place. They argued that "the stars incline, they do not compel," and that therefore free-will existed. God had put signs in the heavens for humankind to see and use. Nevertheless, religion was no friend to astrology during this time in history, and the clergy continued their attacks.

The Loss of Royal Patronage

During the Middle Ages, astrologers had held relatively secure position as private consultants to kings and nobility. But as the fabric of the provincial medieval world was torn apart and the commercially-oriented world of the Renaissance came into being, astrologers were freed from their supporting ties to a single patron.

The printing press created the possibility of serving a greater audience, and soon astrological almanacs were being published, the predecessors of some still in print today. Astrologers soon found themselves competing with one another for popularity. They made predictions for every major planetary configuration, and each astrologer claimed to be more accurate than others. As would be expected, the most outrageous and vocal astrologers were heard and the more cautious were not. For example, in February 1524, all the visible planets were grouped in the sign Pisces. Several years before this event, predictions of a great flood began to appear, and competing astrologers hurled insults at each other. The more sober astrologers did not predict a flood, but they were overshadowed by the drama of the more extreme predictions. Though it was an unusually wet year, the predicted flood did not occur, and astrologers in general suffered discredit in the eyes of the public.

By the mid-17th century the practice of astrology had changed dramatically. Most full-time astrologers were peddling their services in big cities, especially London, or were publishing almanacs. Some, like the great astrologer William Lilly, were very successful. Lilly was consulted by royalty and members of Parliament. But in an age where few people knew their birth times, most of the astrology practiced was horary astrology (answering questions using a chart cast for the time that the client poses the query). More a form of divination than an exact science, horary astrology was even more out of step than natal astrology with the big happenings in the newly emerging scientific community. The new science of astronomy and the practice of astrology had begun to part ways.

The Split Between Astrology and Astronomy

For fifteen hundred years, astrology had been supported by the theories of Ptolemy and Aristotle. Ptolemy had said that the earth lay at the center of the universe, and the planets orbited the earth in complex cycles. In 1543, Copernicus published a manuscript suggesting that the Sun, not the earth, was at the center. While Ptolemy's model could actually predict a planet's future position with some degree of accuracy, Copernicus' model worked better and it became gradually more accepted as the best model. When Ptolemy's astronomical theory was rejected, his astrology was also.

The same thing happened to Aristotle's teachings, partly because of discoveries made by Tycho Brahe. Tycho was a Danish astrologer who, upon finding glaring errors in the planetary tables of his day, devoted his life to making accurate measurements of the planets and stars. He was interested in astrology early in life and consistently defended it, maintaining that accurate astrological analysis was not possible without accurate observation of the heavens. He acquired the patronage of the Danish king, who consulted him on astrological matters such as his sons' horoscopes. Tycho also made accurate predictions regarding the weather and political changes. Today, Tycho is regarded as the founder of modern observational astronomy; science books fail to stress his original astrological motivations.

Tycho was one of the first to report on the New Star of 1572, a supernova that appeared suddenly and lasted for over a year. Tycho's meticulous observations led him to conclude that the new star was located in what was previously considered the unchanging sphere of the fixed stars. Later, in 1577, he noted that a comet had cut through what people believed were solid crystalline spheres of the separate heavens.

Ancient authorities had declared that such things were impossible. Aristotle had postulated a series of heavens above the earth with forces emanating from the highest to the lowest. This notion had provided a theory of how the planets and stars could influence earthly life. This line of reasoning became unacceptable when Tycho's discoveries about the supernova and comet proved that Aristotle's model of the universe was "wrong." Theories that had for centuries made astrology explainable to intellectuals were now being discredited. Worse yet, the discrediting was being led by the most scientific astrologers of the time.

Traditional notions of the nature of the heavens were further upset by the appearance of another supernova in 1604 and by Galileo's discovery of the moons orbiting Jupiter in 1609. Trained only to read horoscopes, most astrologers were unprepared to offer explanations. Only those who had strong technical interests (like Tycho) could address these problems. It was these very technicians who were altering the formerly close relationship between astronomy and astrology.

Following up on Tycho's work was Johannes Kepler, the first to mathematically describe the solar system as we know it today. But Kepler was also an accomplished astrologer who made some very accurate weather predictions and political forecasts. It was Kepler who, in response to the critics of astrology, said "don't throw out the baby with the bath water." He knew that astrology should be updated but, like Tycho, put most of his energy into solving the great astronomical problems of his time. What few people know about this great "first modern astronomer," is that even while Kepler's work made Copernicus' theory a scientific truth, he was guided by astrological ideas. For example, he developed a theory of the harmonies formed by the orbital velocities of the planets, part of his attempt to compose a grand synthesis of mathematics, music, astronomy, and astrology.

By the 17th century, the traditional position of the astrologer in society had changed dramatically. The measurement of the heavens had become a separate discipline called astronomy. Kepler had suggested that astrology be reformed, but his reforms were too extreme for most astrologers to accept. He advocated abandoning the zodiac, except as a convenient reference, and placed nearly all his emphasis on the aspects or angles between the planets. Interestingly, Kepler's ideas on astrology have had some impact in the 20th century, particularly on the German schools of Cosmobiology and Uranian astrology, and also on English astrologer John Addey's theory of harmonics.

Other great 17th-century astrologers include John Goad, who wrote a large treatise on astrometeorology. In this work, he correlated the aspects of the planets with the weather in London, Germany, and other parts of the world. He kept a weather diary for thirty years, and attempted to show that a specific weather pattern frequently occurred at the same time as a particular planetary aspect. Unfortunately, modern statistical techniques for analyzing such data were not to be developed for nearly 150 years. Roughly contemporary with John Goad was Morinus, the French astrologer who wrote the *Astrologia Gallica*. While Goad was groping toward a new science of astrology and had adopted some of Kepler's suggested reforms, Morinus summarized all that had come before. The intellectual climate was changing rapidly, and few had time for the past. As astronomers assumed a leading role in the Scientific Revolution, they abandoned the theories and techniques of astrology.

The Rise of Modern Science

The great movement of the 17th century was the rise of modern science. Its founders were pursuing entirely different problems than their medieval forebears. They wanted to measure material things precisely with mathematics, and they wanted to make flawless predictions. To do so, they found it necessary to limit their studies to astronomical, physical, mechanical, and engineering problems. Problems of a human or psychological nature, which astrology had addressed, could not be measured with mathematics, so these were either left to the clergy or ignored.

In the latter part of the 17th century, the major figure in this changing intellectual and scientific mainstream was Sir Isaac Newton. He was the greatest scientist of his time and had a tremendous influence on intellectuals then and for many years afterward -- and he wasn't interested in astrology. What was truly unique about Newton was that he stamped an entirely new philosophy of nature on the Western consciousness.

With his brilliant mathematical solutions to problems of motion (which were based on Kepler's work), Newton essentially validated the argument that the universe was nothing but one big machine, a clockwork universe. He, and others of his period, ceased to ask "why" certain phenomena in nature occurred. They were only concerned with "how." Although Newton's treatment of gravity is now regarded as his greatest achievement, he could only measure it, observe it, and make accurate predictions about it; he couldn't say exactly what gravity was. The implications of this approach led to the notion that if something couldn't be measured, then it had no place in science. Taken further, this approach suggests the idea that nature is to be measured, controlled and dominated, and that Man is separate from Nature. Today we are seeing that the fruits of this approach, i.e., modern technologies, have been both a blessing and a curse.

Newton's role in history (and it was a large one) was to bring into focus a major ideological shift. In the new science, astrology had no place because it couldn't be proven, measured, or manipulated. It was simply not an experimental science. It was an observational study born during a time in history when humanity was seen to be a part of nature. Astrology was incompatible in many respects with the newly emerging science, and it gradually fell out of favor with scientists.

In fairness to astrology, it should be pointed out that if the social sciences, psychology, anthropology, and sociology, had been around during Newton's time (they weren't to be for another two hundred years), they would have also been rejected as candidates for the new science. Today it is mostly statistical analysis that gives scientific credence to the social sciences and to astrology, and in the late 17th century, statistical analysis was still a long way off.

Other Factors in the Decline

Late in the 17th century came more blows to astrology's formerly great prestige. Life in this age was precarious and the clergy had their own explanations for human disasters. They allowed no room for astrology's answers and they took deliberate measures to discredit it. Weakened by their changing socio-economic situation and divided by disagreements on technical matters, astrologers could no longer counter the power of the clergy. Also, the rise of insurance companies, fire companies, and other securities of modern life served to lessen fears of an uncertain future. Astrology became less important when one could make financial or other arrangements to survive a disaster.

By the 18th century, just about the only astrology left was found in the popular almanacs, and even these were being attacked in satirical almanacs by writers like Jonathan Swift. Though still a vital part of rural and seafaring life, astrology had gone underground in most cities in Europe by 1750. Astrology did continue to be practiced in England, however, for a longer period than on the continent.

In summary, between about 1500 and 1750, astrology was discredited but never actually disproved. Slow to adjust to rapidly changing times, it became unfashionable for the humanists, a threat to organized religion, and a burden to the scientists. Another problem was the failure of astrologers to rally around a common theme, to organize and present a united front. We can't be too harsh on them though, they simply found themselves practicing a complex subject in a rapidly changing and disinterested world.

Astrology Today

In some respects, astrology could not advance until modern science paved the way. Because astrology is a complex subject that requires precise mathematical calculations and can only be scientifically demonstrated (so far) with statistics, many modern developments have had to wait for the advent of the computer. The same could be said of medicine, an interpretive discipline that relies on constant improvements in technology. Modern medicine could not have advanced until laboratory work and chemistry came of age.

Today astrology is again on the rise. While it has changed in many ways, it retains many of its traditional elements. The chief difference is in its adaptation to our present culture. Most astrologers today practice natal astrology and use psychological knowledge in their interpretations of birthcharts. To those who understand its possibilities, astrology has much to contribute to our lives in this modern age. As in the ancient past, astrology integrates humankind with nature and gives meaning to seemingly incomprehensible situations. Astrologers and students of astrology need to better understand its history and let the world know of its great and ancient tradition.

Chapter 5:

Planets and Other Points

The computation of an astrological chart is basically a math problem in astronomy, but what comes after the calculation is entirely different. To actually "do" astrology is to use insight and creativity. Interpreting a birthchart involves an understanding of life, the ability to perceive subtle patterns, and the creative blending of a consistently recurring set of symbols. Every birthchart contains the same symbols, but they are arranged in different combinations so that no two charts are exactly the same. Scientists are uncomfortable with astrology partly because the creative interpretation of symbols is different from working with they are used to -- hard facts. Symbolic interpretation is very close to artistic creativity, a long-accepted, non-logical mental process. It is no coincidence that astrologers are often more than casually involved in the arts or music.

There are four main types of astrological symbols. The first are the *Planets* themselves. They are the players, the moving pieces. The word planet comes from the Greek for wanderer, and for astrological purposes this means any moving body, including the Sun and Moon. The second type of symbol involves the angular separations or alignments between the planets. These angles are called the *Aspects* and they show how the planets relate or don't relate to each other. The *Signs* are a third kind of symbol; they modify the basic planetary natures: the Moon is always the Moon, but it functions differently in Libra than it does in Aries. Finally, the *Houses* symbolize the areas of day-to-day life in which the planets find their strongest expression.

The birthchart, or horoscope, is a map of the sky at the time and place of birth. The symbols it contains describe both the internal and external experiences of a person. Each planet is symbolic of a particular function, just as each part of the body is a part of the whole person. The planets can be interpreted as symbols of specific functions on many levels; the physical, psychological, and social levels of being. In the pages ahead we will see how this is so.

Just as each planet is a part of the entire solar system, in astrology, each planet symbolizes a part of a person's entire being. The discussions that follow here will briefly describe how each planet affects personality, and also what people might be like with that planet emphasized in the birthchart. In these instances, "emphasized" means that the planet is located near the horizon or meridian, which are called the angles of the birthchart. As we saw in Chapter 1, the statistical studies of the Gauquelins have demonstrated the strength of planets when they are in such positions.

The Astronomy of the Solar System

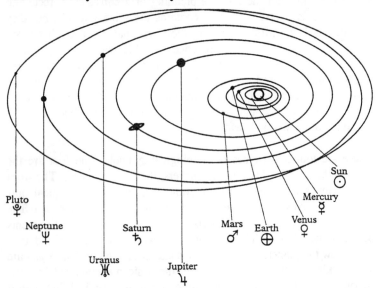

Physical Statistics of the Planets

Planet	Mean Distance from the Sun	Period of Revolution	Diameter
Mercury	36,000,000 mi.	88 days	3,010 mi.
Venus	67,270,000 mi.	225 days	7,650 mi.
Earth	92,955,700 mi.	365.25 days	7,900 mi.
Mars	142,000,000 mi.	687 days	4,200 mi.
Jupiter	483,600,000 mi.	11.86 years	85,000 mi.
Saturn	886,700,000 mi.	29.46 years	71,000 mi.
Uranus	1,782,000,000 mi.	84.01 years	31,000 mi.
Neptune	1,794,000,000 mi.	164.8 years	30,000 mi.
Pluto	4,600,000,000 mi.	248.4 years	2,100 mi.

The Luminaries

The Sun is the most dominant of all objects in the sky, and the Moon is the most dominant by night. In traditional astrology these two are often called the Luminaries or the Lights. In an astrological chart, these two bodies symbolize the most basic energies and needs of life.

The Sun

The Sun is a most important point in an astrological chart. While popular Sun-sign astrology attempts to describe people only from the position of the Sun, such interpretation rings true to some extent because of the tremendous power the Sun has in a birthchart. Astrology sees the entire solar system as an analogy for the self; so the Sun, which is a star at the center of our solar system, symbolizes the center of our lives - our vitality and our will to live. As a center of gravity, the Sun holds the solar system together and keeps the planets from flying off into deep space. Just as the physical Sun maintains the integrity of the solar system, the Sun in the horoscope indicates the integrity of the human system. Socially, the Sun is symbolic of the father, authority, and benevolent leadership.

Self-worth, self-esteem, and ego-strength are symbolized by the Sun. The Sun in a birthchart also symbolizes the amount of energy available to the person. A strong Sun, as shown by its sign, house, and aspects, or its position close to the horizon or meridian, indicates both physical and ego-strength and a tendency to dominate the environment in a direct way. People born with an emphasized Sun in their birthchart are often motivated to exert their power through a display of leadership. A less directly placed Sun does not necessarily mean that the person is weak, it suggests that power and success will come through less direct means. Frequently, the person behind the scenes is the real person in charge. A powerfully placed Sun is not necessarily better or more successful than others, it just shows that a great deal of energy is more directly available to that person. How that energy is managed is what really makes the difference between success and failure.

Natal astrology draws analogies between astrological symbols and parts of the body. Each planet rules the body parts that perform the function that the planet represents. The Sun, associated with vitality and integrity, symbolizes the heart which keeps the body alive, and the spine, which gives it form. Without the Sun, life could not exist.

The Moon

The Moon symbolizes interests, responses, reactions, feelings and instincts. While the Sun is the focal point of the vitality and integrity of the self, the Moon is the focus of the security and nourishment needs. People with an emphasized Moon are typically sensitive, nurturing, and protective. The Moon is also a feminine symbol, specifically the female as mother and prime nurturer. On the most basic levels, satis-faction for the Moon is oral gratification, a need that must be met soon after being born. Immediately after birth, instincts move the infant to seek the security of the mother's breast. The Moon signifies this instinctive need to nourish oneself, and may be linked in later life to oral fixations like overeating and smoking. The Moon appears to be a dominant influence during the first two years of life, and corresponds in many respects to Freud's oral stage. Anatomically, the Moon corresponds to the mouth, stomach, breasts, and womb.

The Moon is a point in the chart that symbolizes subconscious functioning. It is symbolic of an older portion of the brain which generates actions taken without thought. The Moon represents the pre-verbal mind which is inaccessible to reason. It is symbolic of the brain's right hemisphere, the half of the brain that thinks holistically and intuitively. The Moon is thus an important factor in understanding non-rational habits and behaviors.

The position of the Moon in a birthchart shows a person's natural interests and their "instinctive" response to something. (For example, people listen to a particular type of music because there is something in it to which they react.) The Moon also signifies a person's characteristic emotional response. Some people respond to a stimulus dramatically, some tend to suppress their feelings, and others might respond in a creative and balanced manner. It's all shown by the Moon in the birthchart.

The Inner Planets

In astrology, Mercury, Venus, and Mars are often grouped together as the inner planets. In the solar system they are close to the earth and physically small: Venus is almost exactly the same size as the earth, Mars a bit smaller, and Mercury smaller yet. Along with the Moon, these planets represent functions needed by the individual to cope with life's daily demands. They are considered "personal planets" in that they symbolize important aspects of one's own unique personality.

Mercury

Mercury is symbolic of mental activity and the use of language; it is the planet of thinking and communication. It is linked to the brain's left hemisphere, which is logical, analytical, and literal. The Mercury part of the mind is concerned with knowledge and rational problem-solving, both of which require the ability to use symbols and to manipulate ideas and things. Those with Mercury emphasized in the birth chart tend to be talkers, readers, writers, and thinkers.

Ancient traditions often associated the planet Mercury with teachers and bringers of knowledge. The Egyptians linked their god Thoth to Mercury, and the Romans called Mercury the messenger of the gods. From this perspective, Mercury is the planet that symbolizes the movement of information from one place to another. This movement can also be expressed in other ways. Persons with an emphasized Mercury often become associated with some form of transportation, either as a career or an interest. Socially, Mercury is symbolic of those who connect others: lawyers, secretaries, messengers, drivers, etc.

On the physical level, Mercury corresponds to the nervous system, the network that moves information through the body. A negatively emphasized Mercury can correlate with an overworked nervous system, chronic talking, or smoking. A positively emphasized Mercury often correlates with outstanding speech, productive writing, and some serious jogging or bicycle riding.

Venus

Venus is the planet of socialization, relationship, love, courtship, and mating. It symbolizes desire and attraction, interactions with others, and the need to get along with them. A person with an emphasized Venus is likely to be very interested in love and partnering, and will probably make key life decisions around such issues.

Venus also signifies the need for harmony and balance in nature, art, and relationships. Venus is a refining planet and is symbolic of the human striving for a better life, rather than a return to the animal state. Social harmony, social stability, a sense of equality, and a sense of civilization and culture are all linked to Venus. The position of Venus in the birthchart also shows what a person values -- in art, music and other people. Venus is traditionally a feminine symbol. While the Moon is the mother, Venus depicts the beautiful and sexually desirable aspect of femininity.

In the body, Venus corresponds to several internal organs. The kidneys not only filter and purify the blood, they also maintain the stability of its composition. The parathyroid glands also perform a balancing and regulating function. The venous system, unlike the arteries, carries blood back to the heart. Venus is also associated with the female sex organs, particularly the ovaries.

Mars

Mars symbolizes self-preservation, survival, assertiveness, dominance, and territoriality. Crude but to the point, it is the planet of war, combat, and sharp pointed objects. Soldiers, boxers, and firefighters will have an emphasized Mars. Mars is the planet of self-interest and the striving for personal power. Whereas Venus is the planet of the grower, Mars is the planet of the hunter. Mars is a masculine planet symbolic of the male as warrior.

Physiologically, Mars rules the muscles, which empower the body and allow it to move about. Control of one's muscles is needed in order to be autonomous and independent of others. In many ways, Mars could be associated with Freud's anal stage of development, with its emphasis on toilet training. Mars also rules the arteries and the blood itself. Other parts of the body associated with Mars are the male sex glands, and the adrenal gland, which is activated when one's survival is threatened.

A Psychological Model for the Inner Planets

The psychological functions of the inner planets and the Moon can be understood as key points in a hypothetical model of the self. The Sun represents the life force itself and stands at the center. Radiating from this center are four spokes, much like the four directions. The Moon stands at one point and represents the subconscious mind and the oral stage of development. Opposite to the Moon stands Mercury, representing the conscious mind and the language-using stage of human development. At opposite points on the other axis are Mars and Venus. Mars represents the muscle-control and power stage of development, Venus represents the social and sexual stage of development. Freud would recognize this as a model that contains his oral, anal, and genital stages of human development.

This model, based on original ideas from Dr. Timothy Leary, suggests several things. First, and very much in line with Freud's model, it suggests that humans develop in stages that follow the order Moon,

Mars, Mercury, Venus. The Moon stage, which is pre-verbal, extends from birth to about 2 years. During this time, our feelings and our unconscious needs determine how we move forward in life. At about 2 years of age, just when Mars has completed one full cycle since birth, the Mars stage begins. During this period we learn to control our muscles and to assert our power. The "terrible two's" set in during this Mars stage. At about 5 years of age the Mercury stage is dominant. We begin school at this time and learn to use words and language. Between age 12 and 16 Venus is the dominant influence and we confront our sexuality and learn important social lessons.

Another implication of this model is that we take our key imprints for each stage during the time that it is active. For example, we learn how to get what we want for ourselves during the Mars period. If our experiences during this time were difficult, then our "Mars imprint" might need further development later on in life. If the Moon, Mercury, Mars, or Venus are stressfully configured in a birth chart, it may suggest difficulties in each corresponding stage of childhood. It is possible to use astrology to provide valuable information to parents and educators concerning the development of children.

The Asteroids

Until about two hundred years ago, astrologers used just seven planets, those discussed so far plus Jupiter and Saturn. But since that time, three other planets and a number of smaller bodies such as asteroids have been discovered. In our solar system, the gap between Mars and Jupiter is filled with thousands of asteroids. One cosmological theory holds that the asteroids are fragments of an exploded planet; another, that they are the components of a planet that never consolidated. Some astrologers place asteroids in birthcharts and are exploring their potential as symbols of very particular psychological functions.

Four of the largest asteroids, Ceres, Pallas, Juno, and Vesta, were discovered within a few years of each other at the beginning of the 19th century. These four appear to represent specific aspects of the female archetype represented by the Moon and Venus in general. Ceres has to do with nurturing and agriculture. Pallas is intellectual and has to do with feminine crafts, weaving, and pattern perception. Juno is linked to women's arts, female decoration, and female power. Vesta has to do with dedication, celibacy, sacrifice, and service. Prominence of one or more of these asteroids in a birth chart suggests a concern with these issues.

Jupiter and Saturn

Beyond Mars are the two largest planets in the solar system, Jupiter and Saturn. Each is many times larger than Mercury, Venus, and Mars combined. Jupiter is so big that it is just short of being a star and generating its own light. In astrology, these two planets symbolize our adaptation to the larger social reality around us, in contrast to the inner planets, which are more personal and descriptive of the individual self. Together, Jupiter and Saturn symbolize the way we relate to the larger human community in which we live.

Jupiter and Saturn take much longer to orbit the Sun than do the inner planets. The Moon spends 2.5 days in each sign of the zodiac, Mercury around three weeks, Venus about a month, and Mars about six weeks. In contrast, Jupiter spends about a year in each sign, and Saturn 2.5 years. In both size and motion, Jupiter and Saturn have a very different nature than the inner planets, and this is reflected in their observed astrological effects.

Jupiter

Jupiter is the planet of growth, but also of proper timing and regulation. It is associated with acquisition, whether this be intellectual, material, or physical. People with an emphasized Jupiter are often intellectual seekers, information collectors, money-makers, or they may simply be physically large. Jupiter represents the urge to expand one's horizons via traveling or learning. It has to do with the larger view of things, views developed in the fields of philosophy, religion, and legal studies. Socially, Jupiter represents generous and benevolent persons, judges, ministers, and speculators.

Jupiter is also traditionally the planet of luck, which is essentially a matter of timing -- being in the right place at the right time. The ancients considered Jupiter the most beneficial planet of all. However, too much of something can be as detrimental as too little. In the body, Jupiter is linked to the liver, the largest organ, and to the posterior lobe of the pituitary gland, which regulates growth. Jupiter is the planet that is active as an astrological force behind habitual excesses, over-production, and obesity.

Saturn

Saturn is the last of the visible planets known to the ancients, and prior to just 200 years ago, it marked the outer edge of the solar system. Saturn is the planet of limits, boundaries, and barriers. It symbolizes laws, rules and regulations, and the need to establish and conform to realistic perspectives. Whereas Jupiter represents an outgoing energy, Saturn represents a force that contracts. In society, Saturn symbolizes hard workers, realists, farmers, distant authorities, law-makers, and government officials.

People with an emphasized Saturn are often serious, hard-working, goal-driven, and motivated by established standards. Status and reputation are important to the Saturn type. As the planet of responsibility, it can often weigh heavily on a person, leading to feelings of duty and obligation. Saturn represents the need to consolidate and make secure, in terms of both ideas and materials. Anatomically, Saturn rules the bones, which are the hard parts that give the body a definite structure, and the skin, which defines the visible outer limit of the body.

Chiron: A Transitional Object

In 1977, astronomer Charles Kowal discovered what appeared to be a minor planet orbiting between Saturn and Uranus. In one part of its elliptical orbit, this body gets closer to the Sun than Saturn; and in another part, it is farther from the Sun than Uranus ever gets. The orbit of this newly discovered object is representative of a link between the last known planet of the ancients with the first of the modern, outer planets, and this gives it a unique place in the astrological system of planetary symbols.

Astronomers soon named Kowal's new object Chiron, after the king of the centaurs. Although these creatures were part human, they were beasts below the waist, so the centaurs were noted for their savagery and lust. But Chiron was the exception: a teacher and a wounded healer. The consensus of many independent astrological investigators seems to be that the planet Chiron symbolizes several issues including health, healing (chiropractic), disabilities, and also teaching and learning in general. Astrologers also note its isolation from the other asteroids; Chiron symbolizes the independent and solitary qualities of a maverick. In 1988, astronomical research determined that Chiron was beginning to exhibit some of the characteristics of a comet. This unexpected transformation appears to be leading astronomers towards a better understanding of the smaller bodies in our solar system.

The Outer Planets

The three outer planets, Uranus, Neptune, and Pluto, were discovered by telescope. Except for Uranus, which can be seen only under ideal conditions by those with very sharp eyes, these planets are beyond the range of our normal human senses. Astrologically, they symbolize forces that are capable of changing both the individual and the community. They represent the disruptive forces that occur from time to time in a person's life, in the lives of a generation, or in the life of a community. They move so slowly that entire generations have Pluto or Neptune in the same sign at birth. The location óf these planets in a person's birthchart indicates his or her capacity to change, or to be an agent of change. Astrologers have noted that historical events occurring at the time these planets were discovered seem to correlate with their astrological meaning.

Uranus

Uranus was the first of the three outer planets to be discovered. It was unexpectedly sighted in 1781 by the astronomer William Herschel while he was exploring the heavens with a telescope in his backyard. The discovery took place as the American Revolution ended and the French Revolution began. These disruptive events transformed society and have been models for revolutions ever since. The year 1781 also marked the time when the Industrial Revolution became self-perpetuating, and it was also the year that a human left the ground for the first time in a hot-air balloon. Astrologers note that most of our modern political, technical, and industrial realities had their origins around the time that Uranus was discovered.

Astrologically, Uranus symbolizes discovery, technology, instability, and change. It often acts suddenly and unpredictably, disturbing the normal flow of events. It symbolizes advanced technology, invention, ingenuity, deviation, and experiment. Uranus is often described as a higher octave of Mercury because it appears to operate on an extremely mental level. Like Mercury, it is linked to the nervous system, but it is also considered the ruler of the pineal gland, which lies near the brain. Psychologically, Uranus represents the will, the focused intent of a person. People with an emphasized Uranus are often stubborn, rigid, and original characters who may not harmonize with others due to their strong sense of independence. Socially, Uranus represents individualists, reformers, rebels, inventors, and people with an interest in socially transforming technology and electronics.

Neptune

Strange coincidences, dis-information, and chaos are some of Neptune's astrological properties. The circumstances of Neptune's discovery appear to have correlations with this planet's astrological effect. Neptune was sighted in 1846 by two astronomers working independent of each other under confusing and controversial circumstances. At the time of Neptune's discovery, the world saw the introduction of ether as an anesthetic, the development of photography, the rise of Spiritualism, the beginnings of a decadent movement in the arts, and the publication of the seminal works on communism by Karl Marx. Darwinism, a major belief system of the last 150 years, was also becoming an influence on thought at this time.

Like Uranus, Neptune has something to do with vision and movement toward the future, but it operates on the level of the feelings and instincts. Uranus is super-mental and willful, but Neptune is super-sensitive and psychic. Neptune is the spiritual and artistic high, a state of mind where distinctions do not exist. Uranus makes for sharp distinctions: black and white, positive and negative. Neptune represents a dissolving force, where everything blends into everything else, and this can produce chaos. In some respects, Neptune is said to be a higher octave of the Moon, though some would also say Venus.

People with an emphasized Neptune are typically idealistic, artistic, poetic, dreamy, psychic, and imaginative. They usually base crucial life decisions entirely on their feelings and they often sacrifice their lives to another person, or to an ideal. Their philosophical or religious beliefs rule their lives and drive them to do what they can to bring the ideal into reality. With Neptune there is an instinct to lose one's ego, to sacrifice for the greater good, to become selfless, or seek a unified state of consciousness. These persons may be complex, but they are the ones who move humanity towards the future. Socially, Neptune symbolizes artists, visionaries, romantics, spiritualists, psychics, addicts of all sorts, and masters of deception.

Pluto

Pluto marks the outermost limit of the known solar system. This planet was discovered in 1930, the time of the stock market crash, the rise of Hitler, and the powerful underworld of organized crime. The world was in crisis, but out of this crisis a global society emerged. A major force in creating the global society was television, a medium for the masses that was developed around the time of Pluto's discovery. When television becomes linked to the Internet, Pluto's potential in this medium will have been realized. Pluto is less of a personal planet and much more a planet of mass society and large populations in general.

Pluto is physically small, but its astrological influence is great. Simply put, Pluto rules survival itself and the crises of death and regeneration. It symbolizes the power of inevitable transformations, beginnings and endings, birth and death. It rules sex and reproduction, the means by which life regenerates itself and "survives" beyond death. In Plutonian matters, the needs of the species outweigh the needs of the individual. Death makes room for birth and the community lives on.

People with an emphasized Pluto tend to take life seriously and some will react to challenging events as if their very lives were at stake. Others find fulfillment in activities that change and transform the world around them, or they may be concerned with eliminating that which is no longer useful. In the body, Pluto is associated with the sex glands, eliminative organs, and possibly with the DNA found in cells.

Pluto is also associated with hidden things, secrets, and the dark. Like Mars, it symbolizes the power urge, but Pluto's power is more subtle. Whereas Mars rules hand-to-hand combat, Pluto rules psychological warfare, espionage, and nuclear power. A negative Pluto type can be obsessive, jealous, possessive, demanding, domineering, and over-whelming,. Because it is the power and survival of the group that is at issue under Pluto, this planet works best for people who have learned to trust and share. Socially, Pluto is symbolic of people involved with networking, the corporate world, taxation, insurance, and banking.

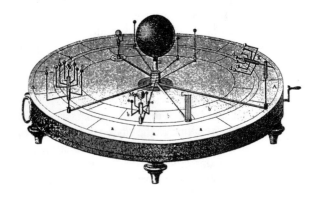

☉ Sun: The Center

Physical: The heart and the spine, the life of the body, physical strength and vitality, the will to live.

Psychological: The need for attention, ego-strength, self-esteem, primary motivations, self-integration.

Social: The hero, the authority, the father, leaders, rulers, male energies in general.

☽ Moon: The Reactor

Physical: The mouth, the stomach, the womb and breasts.

Psychological: Moods and feelings, the subconscious mind, the right brain, instinctive responses and habits, interests, protective urges, the need to nurture or be nurtured.

Social: Family, relations based on feelings, parenting, mother figures, herd (or hive) consciousness, the general public, female energies in general.

☿ Mercury: The Thinker and Communicator

Physical: The nervous system, the left brain, the eyes, the hands, breathing, the lungs.

Psychological: mental activity, mind, rationalizations, relativism, coordination, adaptability, expression.

Social: Communications (speech, writing, translation, etc.), mobility and transportation (cars, bikes, planes), agents, go-betweens.

♀ Venus: The Lover

Physical: The kidneys, veins, female reproductive organs.

Psychological: Attractions, love, romance, courtship, mating, relationship skills, cooperation with others.

Social: Art, beauty, artistic taste, culture, evaluation, balance, peace, negotiations, agreements, marriage, consultants, counselors.

♂ Mars: The Warrior

Physical: The muscles, blood and arteries, and the male sex organs, cuts, bruises, burns.

Psychological: initiative, self-assertion, aggression, personal power, establishment of domain, self-preservation, impulse, rage, passion.

Social: Activity, construction, competition, conflict, war.

♃ **Jupiter:** The Growth Provoker

Physical: The hips, thighs, sciatic nerve, liver, and posterior pituitary gland.

Psychological: Confidence, positive, optimism, humor, generosity, risk-taking, liberal, broad-minded, tolerant.

Social: Growth and increase, overpopulation, exaggeration, volume, abundance, wealth.

♄ **Saturn:** The Limiter

Physical: Bones, teeth, the skeleton, knees, the skin.

Psychological: self-control, restraint, discipline, endurance, patience, persistence, organization, realism, frugality.

Social: Rules and regulations, structure and form, permanence, authority figures, restriction, contraction, separation, obstacles, delays.

♅ **Uranus:** The Deviator

Physical: The ankles, nervous system, and pineal gland.

Psychological: The will, individualism, eccentricity, independence, mental instability, tension, irregularities.

Social: Reforms, rebellions, revolution, anarchy, invention, originality, change, experimentation.

♆ **Neptune:** The Idealist

Physical: The feet, lymphatic system, and thalamus.

Psychological: Dreams, psychic experiences, altered states of consciousness, emotions, hyper-sensitivity, anxiety.

Social: Idealism, socialism, refinement, sensitivity, confusion, lack of distinctions, dreams, drugs, myths, the spiritual.

♇ **Pluto:** The Transformer

Physical: The eliminative and reproductive organs, DNA.

Psychological: Psychic disturbances, territorialism, sexual urges, compulsions, intensity, the need to change oneself.

Social: Power, domination, transformation, crisis, renewal, elimination, purification, death and rebirth, regeneration.

The Ephemeris

Astrologers use a table of planetary positions called an ephemeris to locate planets for any given day. An ephemeris lists the daily position of each planet at midnight or noon in Greenwich, England. In order to determine the position of a planet at a time other than midnight or noon Greenwich Mean Time (GMT or UT), astrologers perform simple mathematical interpolations. Below is a sample page from the *American Ephemeris*, published by Astro Communications Services.

LONGITUDE   JANUARY 2000

DAY	SID.TIME	☉	☽	TRUE Ω	☿	♀	♂	♃	♄	♅	♆	♇
	h m s	° ′ ″	° ′ ′	° ′	° ′	° ′	° ′	° ′	° ′	° ′	° ′	° ′
1 Sa	6 39 31	9♑ 51 32	7♊ 17 33	3♌R59.0	1♉ 6.7	0♐ 57.7	27♏ 34.3	25♈ 14.0	10♉R24.3	14≈ 47.0	3♒ 10.7	11♐ 27.4
2 Su	6 43 48	10 52 42	19 18 59	3 55.9	2 40.1	2 10.2	28 21.1	25 16.4	10 23.1	14 50.0	3 12.9	11 29.5
3 M	6 47 44	11 53 52	1♋ 13 16	3 52.1	4 13.8	3 22.8	29 7.6	25 19.1	10 22.0	14 53.0	3 15.0	11 31.6
4 Tu	6 51 41	12 55 2	13 3 35	3 48.3	5 47.8	4 35.5	29 54.1	25 21.9	10 21.1	14 56.1	3 17.2	11 33.7
5 W	6 55 38	13 56 13	24 52 38	3 44.8	7 22.2	5 48.2	0♐40.7	25 25.0	10 20.2	14 59.2	3 19.4	11 35.8
6 Th	6 59 34	14 57 24	6♌ 42 41	3 42.0	8 56.9	7 1.0	1 27.2	25 28.2	10 19.4	15 2.3	3 21.5	11 37.8
7 F	7 3 31	15 58 35	18 35 44	3 40.1	10 32.0	8 13.9	2 13.8	25 31.7	10 18.8	15 5.3	3 23.7	11 39.9
8 Sa	7 7 27	16 59 45	0♍ 33 38	3D 39.2	12 7.5	9 26.8	3 0.3	25 35.3	10 18.3	15 8.6	3 25.9	11 41.9
9 Su	7 11 24	18 0 55	12 38 16	3 39.3	13 43.3	10 39.7	3 46.8	25 39.1	10 17.9	15 11.8	3 28.1	11 43.9
10 M	7 15 20	19 2 6	24 51 41	3 40.0	15 19.6	11 52.7	4 33.3	25 43.2	10 17.6	15 15.0	3 30.4	11 45.8
11 Tu	7 19 17	20 3 15	7♎ 16 13	3 41.2	16 56.3	13 5.8	5 19.8	25 47.4	10 17.4	15 18.3	3 32.6	11 47.8
12 W	7 23 13	21 4 24	19 54 27	3 42.5	18 33.5	14 18.9	6 6.3	25 51.8	10D 17.3	15 21.5	3 34.8	11 49.7
13 Th	7 27 10	22 5 33	2♏ 49 9	3 43.5	20 11.1	15 32.0	6 52.8	25 56.4	10 17.3	15 24.8	3 37.0	11 51.6
14 F	7 31 7	23 6 40	16 3 1	3R 44.1	21 49.2	16 45.2	7 39.3	26 1.2	10 17.3	15 28.1	3 39.3	11 53.5
15 Sa	7 35 3	24 7 47	29 38 14	3 44.2	23 27.7	17 58.4	8 25.7	26 6.1	10 17.7	15 31.4	3 41.5	11 55.4
16 Su	7 39 0	25 8 54	13♐ 36 1	3 43.8	25 6.8	19 11.6	9 12.2	26 11.3	10 18.1	15 34.7	3 43.8	11 57.2
17 M	7 42 56	26 10 0	27 55 55	3 43.2	26 46.3	20 24.9	9 58.6	26 16.6	10 18.6	15 38.0	3 46.1	11 59.0
18 Tu	7 46 53	27 11 5	12♑ 35 22	3 42.4	28 26.4	21 38.3	10 45.0	26 22.1	10 19.2	15 41.3	3 48.3	12 0.8
19 W	7 50 49	28 12 9	27 29 26	3 41.6	0♒ 7.0	22 51.6	11 31.4	26 27.8	10 19.9	15 44.7	3 50.6	12 2.6
20 Th	7 54 46	29 13 13	12♒ 30 59	3 41.1	1 48.1	24 5.1	12 17.8	26 33.7	10 20.7	15 48.1	3 52.9	12 4.4
21 F	7 58 42	0♒ 14 16	27 31 35	3D 40.9	3 29.7	25 18.5	13 4.1	26 39.7	10 21.7	15 51.5	3 55.1	12 6.1
22 Sa	8 2 39	1 15 18	12♓ 22 34	3 40.8	5 11.8	26 32.0	13 50.4	26 45.9	10 22.7	15 54.9	3 57.4	12 7.8
23 Su	8 6 36	2 16 20	26 56 19	3 40.9	6 54.4	27 45.5	14 36.7	26 52.3	10 23.9	15 58.3	3 59.7	12 9.5
24 M	8 10 32	3 17 20	11♈ 7 15	3 41.0	8 37.4	28 59.0	15 23.0	26 58.8	10 25.1	16 1.7	4 2.0	12 11.1
25 Tu	8 14 29	4 18 21	24 52 19	3R 41.1	10 20.9	0♑ 12.6	16 9.3	27 5.5	10 26.5	16 5.1	4 4.3	12 12.8
26 W	8 18 25	5 19 21	8♉ 10 57	3 41.0	12 4.9	1 26.2	16 55.3	27 12.3	10 28.0	16 8.6	4 6.5	12 14.4
27 Th	8 22 22	6 20 20	21 4 42	3D 41.0	13 49.1	2 39.9	17 41.8	27 19.4	10 29.6	16 12.0	4 8.8	12 16.0
28 F	8 26 18	7 21 18	3♊ 36 40	3 41.0	15 33.7	3 53.6	18 28.0	27 26.5	10 31.3	16 15.5	4 11.1	12 17.5
29 Sa	8 30 15	8 22 17	15 50 56	3 41.1	17 18.4	5 7.3	19 14.1	27 33.9	10 33.1	16 18.9	4 13.4	12 19.0
30 Su	8 34 11	9 23 14	27 52 3	3 41.5	19 3.3	6 21.0	20 0.3	27 41.4	10 35.0	16 22.4	4 15.6	12 20.5
31 M	8 38 8	10♒ 24 11	9♋ 44 42	3♌ 42.1	20♒ 48.1	7♑ 34.8	20♐ 46.4	27♈ 49.0	10♉ 37.0	16≈ 25.9	4♒ 17.9	12♐ 22.0

Lunar and Planetary Nodes

The Moon's nodes have long been in common use by astrologers. The nodes are not physical objects, they simply mark the intersection of the plane defined by the Moon's orbit with the orbital plane of the earth. Since the intersection of two planes produces a straight line, there are really two nodal points commonly called the north node and south node. Since none of the planets share exactly the same orbital plane as the earth, each planet has its own set of nodes.

The Moon's nodes are generally interpreted as sensitive points in the birthchart that symbolize connections with family, friends, and other nurturing associations. In Hindu astrology, the north node (Rahu) and the south node (Ketu) are so important that they are elevated to the status of planets.

The Part of Fortune

The part of fortune is one of a large number of "parts" determined with horoscopic geometry and planetary positions. The part of fortune, for example, is located by adding the phase angle of the Sun and Moon to the Ascendant (see Chapter 8). If the Moon was 90 degrees ahead of the Sun, then the part of fortune is 90 degrees ahead of the Ascendant. Although a totally derived point in the zodiac, it is held to be symbolic of opportunity and possible good fortune. There are many other parts derived from various planet combinations and determined by a similar formula. Traditionally, the parts for night births and day births were calculated differently.

Hypothetical Planets

During the 20th century, some astrologers have proposed the existence and astrological use of planets that have not been verified astronomically. The orbits and symbolic nature of many of these hypothetical planets have been determined on the basis of astrological observation alone. Most of them are said to have orbits beyond that of Pluto. While most astrologers do not use them in their work, the Hamburg School of Astrology in Germany, also known as Uranian Astrology in the U.S., utilizes eight of these hypothetical planets in their methodology. Transpluto, also known as Persephone, is one hypothetical planet whose orbital parameters have been calculated by astronomers but which has not yet been sighted. It is believed by some astrologers to be a feminine planet that symbolizes female maturity, ecological balance, and the dynamics of gender-balanced relationships.

The Fixed Stars

Some astrologers use stars for an expanded interpretation of the horoscope. These stars are called "fixed" because they remain more or less in the same place with respect to the other stars around them. They don't have an orbital motion like the planets. Certain stars such as the "royal stars" (Aldebaran, Regulus, Antares, and Fomalhaut) have been used by astrologers since ancient times. Their degree positions in the zodiac seem to have a definite "charge" to them, and planets located near them appear to gain in power.

The fixed stars do not move relative to each other (except for minor adjustments over thousands of years), but they do exhibit measurable movement relative to the equinoxes and solstices. This motion is called the precession of the equinoxes, whereby the stars move at the rate of about one degree of the zodiac every 72 years. A number of dramatic astrological predictions, based on this slow movement, have involved the movement of a point in a horoscope to one fixed star or another.

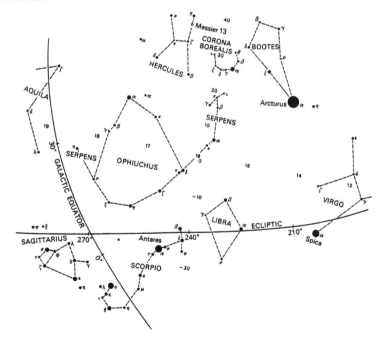

Chapter 6:

Aspects and Alignments

Of the four primary sets of symbols in astrology, planets are clearly the most important. Their positions in the sky and in the horoscope are measured in degrees along the pathway of the Sun that is called the ecliptic. The specific angular separations between the planets, called aspects, take planetary symbolism one step further in that they show linkages and blendings between two or more planets. If the horoscope were an electronic circuit board, the planets would be the transistors and chips, and the aspects would be the wires or metallic tracks that link them.

An aspect is a specific kind of alignment that occurs when two planets are separated by a key geometric angle. The aspects are based on sections of the ecliptic or Sun's path. For example, planets on the ecliptic that are separated by about 90 degrees (one-quarter of the 360-degree circle) are in a square aspect. Those separated by 120 degrees, or a third of a circle, are in a trine aspect, and so forth. While about ten aspects are commonly used by modern astrologers, only two were recognized in ancient Mesopotamia, where astrology originated. These were the conjunction (an angular separation of zero degrees) and the opposition (an angular separation of 180 degrees). Three others, the sextile, square, and trine, were added by the Greeks, who applied their geometry to the astrology of the Near East. Much later, Johannes Kepler, the great astronomer-astrologer, added several minor aspects to the list.

Students of numerology will notice that each of the aspects is based on the division of the circle by a number. In fact, this is one area in which numerology and astrology overlap. It was the Greek astrologers, strongly influenced by the scientist and numerologist Pythagoras, who were behind the development of the aspects. A comparison of the nature of the aspects with traditional numerology will reveal deep similarities.

It is helpful to think of the aspects in terms of vibrations and harmonics. The division of the circle of the zodiac by each number, called the fundamental, produces a specific tone or harmonic. Johannes Kepler understood this and attempted to reform astrology so as to be based around this principle.

The Principal Aspects: Harmonics 1 through 12

Conjunctions

The conjunction is the most powerful aspect between planets. It occurs when two planets occupy the same or nearly the same degree of the zodiac. It represents a division of the 360 degrees of the circle by one. The circle represents completeness, a condition in which all things are the same -- merged and unified. The conjunction of two planets symbolizes a fusion of their principles. For example, Saturn conjunct the Sun suggests that the cold of Saturn is conjoined with the heat of the Sun. Saturn is warmed up, but the Sun is cooled down. The new Moon is actually a conjunction of the Sun and Moon.

Oppositions

Division of the circle by two produces the opposition, where the planets are separated by 180 degrees. With the opposition, the qualities of the planets are not blended as in the conjunction; they are separated yet forced to co-exist. The opposition has mixed qualities and some combinations of planets fare better when in this aspect than others. The full Moon is the opposition between Sun and Moon.

Trines

Division of the circle by three produces the trine, or 120 degrees. Two planets in trine work well together; they are in phase or in balance with each other. Symbolically, the number one is manifestation, two is challenge, and three is harmony. In other words, one is the thesis, two is the antithesis, and three is the synthesis: the resolution of the dialectic, the bridging of the gap. The trine is stable like a triangle. The triangle is such a solid form that bridge-builders often utilize its shape. Three planets spaced equidistant from each other, 120 degrees apart, create what is known as a Grand Trine. This powerful configuration is generally stable and strong, but such extreme stability is not always a good thing because it can indicate resistant to change.

Squares

Division of the circle by four produces the square, or 90 degrees. The square is tense and stressful, yet its demands often result in action and productivity. Although two planets in square are out of phase with each other, this aspect forces the two to work together toward practical ends. In this respect the square is not such a negative aspect. The quarters of the Moon occur when the Sun and Moon are in square.

Four planets in square to each other produce what is called a Grand Cross. This is a particularly tense configuration requiring a constant effort to maintain a balance between the four points. Many people with such a configuration in their charts become stressed, while others are extremely productive and successful.

Quintiles and Biquintiles

Dividing the circle by five produces the quintile, or 72 degrees. Because 72 degrees is harder to spot than multiples of 30 degrees, this aspect is frequently overlooked and therefore not used by many astrologers. Overall, it is a positive aspect that promotes creativity and productivity in a natural way. The biquintile is 144 degrees, or twice the quintile, and has a similar effect.

Sextiles

Division of the circle by six produces the sextile, or 60 degrees. Like the quintile, this aspect is considered positive in that it allows the planets to function together harmoniously. However, it works in less creative and natural ways than does the quintile. The sextile symbolizes possibilities that need work or attention in order to reach completion.

Septiles

Dividing the circle by seven produces the septile, an aspect that is close to 52 degrees plus about 24 minutes. Seven is the first number that does not divide exactly into 360. Numbers that have this property are sometimes called irrational. This strange aspect, rarely used by astrologers in the past because it was hard to calculate (but now no problem with computers), is found in the charts of those who reach for the unattainable. For example, it is frequently found in the charts of those devoted to religion and spirituality.

Semisquares and Sesquiquadrates

Dividing the circle by eight produces the semisquare (or octile), which is 45 degrees. The semisquare is half of a square. Like the square, it symbolizes crisis and it tends to operate practically, directly, and immediately. It is regarded by astrologers as moderately stressful, but potentially productive. The sesquiquadrate (a.k.a. sesquisquare or tri-octile) is 135 degrees, or three times the semisquare. It is very similar to the semisquare.

Continued

Noviles, Deciles, and Elevenths

Division of the circle by nine, ten, and eleven produces aspects that are only rarely used by astrologers. The novile and decile are said to be moderately favorable while the eleventh, the second lowest irrational number, is said to be difficult. The labeling of favorable and difficult is really the product of hard-working astrologers who are pressed by their clients to make black or white judgment calls. The real effects of these subtle aspects are difficult to convey to people not interested in their spiritual evolution. The truth is that no aspect is actually good or bad. Aspects are just what they are and we must do our best with them.

The Semisextile and Quincunx

Division of the circle by twelve produces the semisextile, an aspect of 30 degrees. Since it links adjacent signs of the zodiac, which have very little in common, the effects of this aspect can vary. Most practicing astrologers consider it moderately inharmonious. The quincunx or inconjunct is 150 degrees (five times the semisextile). Its effects are generally considered even more inharmonious than the semisextile.

Parallels and Contraparallels

There are two other aspects that are not measured along the ecliptic and are not based on division of the circle. The parallel occurs when two planets are equidistant from the celestial equator, and both are either north or south. In other words, both planets share the same declination. The contra-parallel occurs when two planets are equidistant from the celestial equator, but one is north and one is south. The parallel tends to work like a conjunction; the contraparallel like an opposition.

Hard vs. Soft Aspects

The opposition, square, semisquare, and sesquiquadrate are all aspects that show a potential for crisis, response, and productivity. These aspects, often called *hard* or *challenging* aspects, are found in the charts of those who struggle for achievement. Great men and women seem to be driven by these powerful aspects which signify the need to balance conflicting planetary energies.

Trines and sextiles are often called *soft* or *harmonious* aspects. People with too many of these are usually not so strongly motivated to resolve challenges and inner tensions, and consequently they tend to be less visibly productive.

Major vs. Minor Aspects

In practice, most astrologers use the conjunction, opposition, trine, square, and sextile as major aspects. These aspects are traditionally known as the *Ptolemaic Aspects*, named after the great astrologer-astronomer Claudius Ptolemy who lived in Egypt during the time of the Roman Empire. Minor aspects include the semisquare and sesquiquadrate, the quintile, the septile, and the semisextile and quincunx. There are also other, even smaller, minor aspects that are used by some astrologers. These include the 16th harmonic, sometimes called the semi-semisquare (22.5 degrees), and the 32nd harmonic (11.25 degrees). These aspects function only when they are exact or very close to exact.

The division of the circle by successively larger numbers creates an infinite number of harmonics or aspects, and each aspect thus created should theoretically have some effect. As the numbers get larger and the aspects become smaller, however, the effect becomes too subtle and the work involved becomes meaningless. Kepler felt that some people respond to minor aspects (or higher harmonics) to a greater degree than others, it was a matter of being sensitive to them.

Applying, Separating, and Orbs

In the preceding discussion, the aspects were considered as exact angular separations between planets. In practice, an exact aspect is very rare. More commonly, two planets may be separated by a figure that is close to, but does not equal, the exact angle. For example, two planets spaced 125 degrees apart are close to the distance of the trine which is 120 degrees. When the relative motions of the planets involved in an aspect are considered in this regard, we can tell if the aspect was exact before birth or afterward. Applying aspects are those that were not yet complete at birth, separating aspects have already formed. For example, if the Moon and Mars were trine each other at birth, but the actual degree of the Moon in its sign was lower than that of Mars, the aspect is applying.

Astrologers regard each aspect as having a range of effect which is called its orb of influence. In general, the orbs for the conjunction and opposition are larger than those for the other aspects. Also the orbs for any aspect involving the Sun or Moon are generally larger than those for the other planets. Although there is no universally agreed upon set of orbs for the aspects, suggested values are given for each aspect in the summary below.

A Summary of the Aspects

Major Aspects

Below are the five traditional (Ptolemaic) astrological aspects in order of strength. Also included are four additional aspects used by most astrologers.

♂ *Conjunction:* 0 degrees or 360 degrees apart. This aspect represents the beginning and end of a cycle and the fusing of the principles of the planets involved in an unconscious way. Its net astrological effect depends on the nature of the planets. Orb: +/- 10 degrees.

♂ *Opposition:* 180 degrees. This aspect marks the midpoint of a cycle. It usually represents a division or a critical turning point. It can mean success as a result of awareness, objectivity, and perspective, or it can imply conflict and separation. It symbolizes the need for understanding. Orb: +/- 10 degrees.

△ *Trine:* 120 degrees. Said to be the most favorable aspect, the trine represents a state of balance and harmony between the planets involved and what they symbolize. Orb: +/- 7 degrees.

☐ *Square:* 90 degrees. This may be the most stressful aspect because it usually demands action or change. It represents the struggle between incompatible elements, and the consequent need for adjustments. Orb: +/- 7 degrees.

✳ *Sextile:* 60 degrees. The sextile, being one-half the value of the trine, has traditionally been regarded as an aspect that presents opportunities that require a little effort. It represents a point of stability in a cycle, and is favorable, but not as strong, as the trine. Orb: +/- 4 degrees.

Minor Aspects

∠ *Semisquare:* 45 degrees. This aspect, being one-half the value of the square, represents a point of friction and agitation that demands a practical response. Orb: +/-3 degrees.

⌐ *Sesquisquare:* 135 degrees. This aspect is three times a semisquare and as such is similar in effect. Orb: +/- 3 degrees.

⊻ *Semisextile:* 30 degrees. This aspect represents the onset of awareness and the blending of different elements. It symbolizes a mild discomfort or instability. Orb: +/- 2 degrees.

⊼ *Quincunx:* 150 degrees. Similar to the semisextile, though possibly stronger and more noticeable. The quincunx symbolizes the awareness of incompatibility, which leads to tradeoffs and compromises. It is also associated with health issues. Orb: +/- 2 degrees.

Midpoints

Planetary positions in a birthchart can be seen as energy vectors pointing outwards from the center in specific directions. When two planets are separated by an aspect, their energies mix -- with a range of possible results. Aspects, then, are a way of interpreting the blending of planetary influences. Another way is to locate the midpoint between any two planets.

To locate a midpoint between two planets you take the sum of two planetary positions and divide by two. Here's an example: The Sun is at 10 degrees of Aries and the Moon is at 10 degrees of Taurus. There are 30 degrees in a sign, so we add 10 for the Sun and 40 for the Moon. Then we take the sum, which is 50, and divide by 2. The Sun/Moon midpoint is at 25 degrees of Aries.

The midpoint of any two planets is a sensitive point in a chart where the energies of the two planets come together in a unique blend. Using the above example, the Sun/Moon midpoint symbolizes the merging of the masculine and feminine principles in the chart. This is a point that says much about a person's relationships with the opposite sex. Very subtle astrological delineations can be made using midpoints, and even aspects to midpoints.

The German Hamburg School of Astrology, known in the United States as Uranian Astrology, utilizes the concept of midpoints extensively. Planetary pictures are symmetrical alignments of planets that are not necessarily in aspect with each other. Groupings of planets that share a common midpoint, or axis, are considered to be very important.

Chapter 7:

Signs of the Zodiac

The zodiac is a division of the ecliptic -- the Sun's path through the sky. The term ecliptic refers to the fact that eclipses can only occur when the Moon is precisely on the Sun's path. Besides the Sun, the Moon and the planets also travel within a few degrees north or south of this path as they move through their cycles. The zodiac of twelve signs used in Western astrology is a Near Eastern creation which most historians believe attained its present form about the 5th century B.C.

Why Twelve Signs?

There are some good reasons why the zodiac is divided into twelve and not eleven or thirteen signs. Astronomically, a year has 365.2422 days, and there are an average of 12.4 Full Moons per year. This means that, depending on when the first full Moon occurred, there could be either twelve or thirteen full Moons in any given year. The cycles of the Sun and Moon do not mesh perfectly.

In early times, humankind looked to the skies for a sense of order. One of the first applications of ancient skywatching was the construction of calendars. The first calendars were based on the Moon's cycle, but lunar calendars are impractical for agricultural pursuits because they require periodic adjustments. A solar calendar is based on the seasons and is very regular. In the search for linkages between lunar and solar cycles, early Near Eastern calendar makers sought round numbers, not fractions, and they ultimately settled on twelve. One practical feature of the number twelve is that it is divisible by two, three, four and six, which is not true of numbers like eleven, thirteen, or fourteen. In other words, twelve contains a large number of small whole number divisors and lends itself to various numerically aesthetic arrangements that facilitate computations. Twelve is a powerful number.

Other cultures have created other ways of dividing the sky. The ancient Chinese used a twenty-eight-fold division based on the cycle of the Moon. These twenty-eight lunar mansions, as they are called, are about thirteen degrees long, the approximate distance traversed by the Moon each day. In India today, lunar mansions are used in addition to a twelve-sign zodiac.

The solar calendar and the twelve primary divisions of the zodiac are astronomical frames of reference created by cultures in the Northern Hemisphere. They are 30-degree spatial sections of the sky, not tangible objects like planets. Our twelve-sign zodiac has a central place in the Western astrological tradition, and nearly every practicing astrologer agrees that the signs do seem to work -- they modify the characteristics of the planets that pass through them. This is probably due to the fact that the tropical zodiac we use today marks stages in the seasonal cycle, the cycle around which living things have adapted.

The Zodiac and the Seasons

In Chapter 1 we discussed two types of zodiac: sidereal zodiacs, which are tied to the constellations, and the tropical zodiac, which has retained the names of the constellations, but is actually defined by the equinoxes. It is the tropical zodiac that is most commonly used in Western astrology today. It starts with the vernal equinox, the place where the Sun is located on March 20th or 21st every year. On this day, the first day that the Sun is in the sign Aries, the Sun rises due East and sets due West. It also rises and sets on the east/west line on the day of the autumnal equinox, which is the first day that the Sun is in the sign Libra. The term equinox refers to the fact that, because the Sun rises due east and sets due west, the days and nights are of equal length (equi-nox means "equal night").

As the days progress following the vernal equinox, the Sun rises further and further to the north of due east. At the summer solstice, the Sun rises at its northernmost rising position, and before beginning its six-month journey further and further south, it appears for several days to rise at this same point. (Thus the term solstice which means "Sun-stand-still.")

The summer solstice marks the beginning of the sign Cancer. At the winter solstice, the Sun rises at its southernmost point and marks the beginning of the sign Capricorn. These positions, which are known in astrology as the cusps or beginnings of the Cardinal signs, create the four quarters of the year, otherwise known as the seasons. This is the basis of all solar calendars. Dividing each of these quarters into three equal parts produces the twelve signs of the zodiac. It is the Sun in its yearly cycle, therefore, that establishes the zodiac.

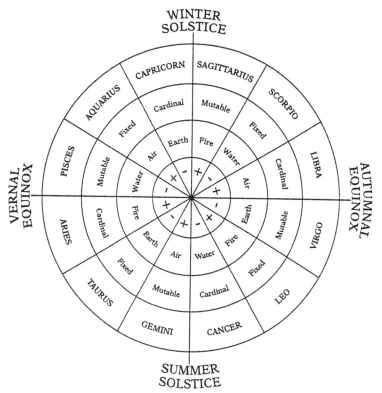

WINTER
SOLSTICE

VERNAL
EQUINOX

AUTUMNAL
EQUINOX

SUMMER
SOLSTICE

The Quadruplicities or Qualities

Aries, Cancer, Libra, and Capricorn are called the Cardinal signs because the Sun enters them at the beginning of each season. After each Cardinal sign comes a Fixed sign, and after each Fixed sign comes a Mutable sign. Then the whole cycle begins again with a Cardinal sign. This grouping of signs is called the Quadruplicities, Crosses, Qualities, or Modes.

Persons born with the Sun in Cardinal signs (Aries, Cancer, Libra, Capricorn) are quick, initiating, busy, natural starters who are often at their best when getting projects off the ground. They are sometimes too restless for work that involves a regular routine. Fixed signs, (Taurus, Leo, Scorpio, Aquarius) are solid, resistant to change, and strive for regularity. They can be enduring, consistent, and sometimes stubborn. Mutable signs (Gemini, Virgo, Sagittarius, Pisces) are changeable, adaptable, and often involved in multiple projects. They tend to be flexible because they can see both sides of an issue.

63

The Triplicities or Elements

Signs are also classified by Element. The fire signs (Aries, Leo, Sagittarius) are spirited, active, and inspired. Earth signs (Taurus, Virgo, Capricorn) are practical, conservative, and concerned with the material world. The Air signs (Gemini, Libra, Aquarius) are mental, communicative, and social. Water signs (Cancer, Scorpio, Pisces) are sensitive, emotional, and intuitive.

The Polarities

Finally, the signs are grouped into two categories called the Polarities. Like a pulse, the sequence of signs in the zodiac alternates between signs of outgoing energies and signs of inturning energies. Fire and Air signs are masculine or Yang, and Earth and Water signs are feminine or Yin. Since the zodiacal signs are arranged in the sequence Fire, Earth, Air, Water, etc., they also alternate masculine, feminine, masculine, feminine, etc. (or +, -, +, -).

The Signs through the Year

Aries, the first sign, begins when the Sun is at the vernal equinox; it symbolizes spring, the seed breaking its shell, the release of stored energy, and the birth of the self. Taurus has to do with substance, materials, possessions, and resources: what there is to work with. Gemini is concerned with information, communication, reaching out and manipulating the environment. Cancer has to do with nurturing, protection, domesticity, home and family; Leo with creativity, drama, the power and glory of the individual; Virgo with criticism, analysis, perfection, and discrimination.

When applied to human life, the first six signs of the zodiac (from the spring to the fall equinox) symbolize the development or evolution of the individual. Aries is self-survival; Taurus is the use of resources and territory; and Gemini gets to know the environment by traveling, learning, and communicating. Cancer establishes the home and family, a base of operations, and a place for centering and protection; Leo masters life and dominates the world; and then Virgo becomes aware of flaws and of the need for adjustment and perfection.

While the first six signs are about the self, the second six are about the self in society. Each sign in the second half of the zodiac can be viewed as a more social manifestation of the opposite sign in the first half. Whereas Aries was the sign of self-encounter, Libra, its opposite, symbolizes basic relationship and cooperation -- the encounter with another. Scorpio has to do with materials, but specifically the materials of relationship, including sex, physical sharing, borrowing and lending. Sagittarius seeks a deeper, wider kind of knowledge than Gemini, traveling to more distant places, learning foreign languages, and coming to an understanding of cultural differences.

Capricorn has to do with finding one's place within the community. Whereas Cancer sought an emotionally secure center in the family, Capricorn seeks security in society through social position, status, and reputation. Aquarius symbolizes friendships and complex social experiments, the cooperation of individuals within groups. Whereas Leo led as an individual, Aquarius is more democratic and seeks to meet power needs through a group. Pisces has to do with the breakdown of social patterns. Whereas Virgo was critical of the self, Pisces is critical of society. It is the sign of the hermit, the monk, the artist, and the psychic, a symbol of the search for a higher social purpose. Both Aquarius and Pisces are signs of change, as if a breakdown were needed before the cycle could begin again at Aries.

Affinities with the Planets

Although the Sun's seasonal cycle defines the signs of the zodiac, the Moon and planets, which orbit in basically the same plane as the Sun, pass through them as well. Traditionally, each planet was said to have a special affinity or resonance with particular signs. These linkages between the signs and the planets, called rulerships, follow a symmetrical pattern. Arranging the signs with the Cancer-Leo cusp at the top of the wheel, the Sun and Moon rule Leo and Cancer respectively, Mercury, the next planet, rules the next two signs on either side, Virgo and Gemini. Venus rules Libra and Taurus, the next two signs. Mars rules Scorpio and Aries, Jupiter rules Sagittarius and Pisces, and Saturn rules Capricorn and Aquarius. Note that this order is the same order as planets arranged by their distance from the Sun. Note also that, except for the Sun and Moon, each planet rules one masculine sign and one feminine sign. This perfect symmetry was destroyed when Uranus, Neptune and Pluto were discovered in the 18th, 19th, and 20th centuries. These outer planets are now regarded as additional, higher-octave rulers of three of the social signs.

Descriptions of the Signs

Below are the glyphs (symbols) and the principal characteristics of each sign with a brief description of how each sign affects the Sun. Following this are brief delineations for the Moon and Ascendant, also important points in the horoscope. You will find the Ascendant explained more fully in Chapter 8. Additional information includes the ruling planet, some keywords, body correspondences, and typical professions for each of the signs.

♈ **Aries** is a fire sign and the first sign of the zodiac. Those born with the Sun here make choices in life that may be daring or pioneering, at least in comparison with their peers. They are generally active, direct, courageous, forceful, and quite impulsive people. They meet the world in an immediate way and take a minimalist approach to things. Aries types like their independence and often prefer to work alone. Many are drawn to wild, untamed places and activities. They can be very constructive when their energies are harnessed, but the same energy can also fuel competitive instincts.

Life Issue: Do I really exist?

The *Moon in Aries* gives quick reactions and a need for excitement. Interest in sports and risk-taking is common with the Moon in this placement. Weaknesses include problems with self-control and a tendency to lose interest in things before bringing matters to a conclusion.

The *Ascendant in Aries* gives a personality that takes the initiative in social matters. Self-interest is strong with this sign and there is a vital need for personal gratification. Those with Aries rising like their personal privacy, and they are often loners or soloists in important areas of their life. They also tend to be good problem solvers and they work quickly and efficiently.

Ruling Planet: Mars

Body: Head, blood, muscles

Professions: Engineering, architecture, athletics, mechanical repair work, the military, construction.

Additional Keywords: Impact. Direct. To the point. Basic. Primitive. Spartan. Bold. Lively. Forceful. Pioneering. The color Red.

♉ **Taurus** is an earth sign that is solid and slow to change. Sun in Taurus is likely to be territorial, possessive, practical, determined, stubborn, beauty-conscious, pleasure-loving, and self-indulgent. There is usually a strong conservative tendency in this sign, at least in terms of self-definition. Taurus likes permanence and security and is easily attracted to money, valuable objects, and land. The Sun in Taurus often occurs in the charts of those who build things or develop systems.

Life Issue: How much do I own?

The *Moon in Taurus* is comfort-driven. People with this Moon sign generally have steady emotions, but they also have strong cravings for pleasures. Habits may be hard to break. Taste in most matters is generally mainstream and conservative. This is a materialistic signature in the chart -- security is found in things of substance.

The *Ascendant in Taurus* confers a strong interest in art and physical beauty. Such people will often work to raise the aesthetic levels around them. This type of personality is quick to establish a standard social routine, but then gets stuck, finding it difficult to adjust or make changes.

Ruling Planet: Venus

Body: Neck and throat

Professions: Fashion and beauty, landscaping, investing, banking, land ownership, cashiering, art, music, design.

Additional Keywords: Solidity. Down to earth. Enduring. Practical. Hard-headed. Natural. Luxury. Sensuous.

♊ **Gemini** is an air sign and likes to be constantly on the move. Sun in Gemini types are quick, changeable, clever, curious, adaptable, intellectual, and communicative. The sign is basically concerned with communications (talk, words, ideas, messages) and transportation (movement, mobility, linkage, connection). Varied experiences and interests lead to an understanding of the relationships between things. The Sun in Gemini is often a jack-of-all-trades.

Life Issue: How many can I have?

The *Moon in Gemini* gives an interest in speaking, writing and teaching. People with the Moon in this sign are often busy with many projects and fully engaged in communicative activities, so they are stretched thin as a result. They tend to rationalize their emotions and prefer relationships that are strong on conversation.

People with the *Ascendant in Gemini* have a lot of nervous energy and are often talkative and sometimes very witty. Their identities seem to be bound up with the themes of communication (phones, computers, books, paperwork) or transportation (cars, bicycles, skating, etc.).

Ruling Planet: Mercury

Body: Nervous system, eyes, left brain, hands, lungs.

Professions: Writing, speaking, communications, computers, teaching, driving, printing, secretarial work, translating.

Additional Keywords: Flexibility. Light. Eclectic. Varied. Adapted to other influences. Neutral. Communicative. Message-oriented. Clever. Slippery.

♋ **Cancer,** a water sign, is motivated by emotional, rather than rational, considerations. Life is driven by the need for a home base, domestic security, the feeling of being at home. Typically, Cancerians are protective, resourceful, conservative, shrewd, sensitive, romantic, imaginative, maternal, and domestic. They are fascinated by the past, both personal and historical, and are often collectors. Cancer is the sign of the mother, and also of nourishment and eating. It is a sensitive sign, not very comfortable with criticism.

Life Issue: What does home feel like?

The *Moon in Cancer* indicates a personable nature with strong maternal or protective instincts. People with the Moon in this sign have prominent issues with the care of others, both in personal matters and professionally. There is often an attraction to water and a desire to live near it.

Those with the *Ascendant in Cancer* are very sensitive to the external world and can be quite touchy. Some even have highly sensitive skin. They interact intensely with the world around them. Their identity is typically built around care, concern, and preservation.

Ruling Planet: Moon

Body: Mouth, stomach, breasts, womb

Professions: Public relations, banking, cooking, gardening, restaurant and hotel work, food industry, real estate, homemaking.

Additional Keywords: Security. Homey. Traditional. Mother Nature. Collectible. Antique. Silver. The Sea. The Country.

♌ **Leo,** is a fire sign and one of the more prominent and dominating signs of the zodiac. People with the Sun in Leo are usually creative, dramatic, proud, authoritative, fond of entertainment or entertaining, lavish, forgiving, and generous. Leo is a sign that is really about self-esteem and self-worth issues, though most people wouldn't know this from the dramatic and seemingly confident presentation of the self that seems to go with this sign. Leo produces romantic lovers, artists, and also parents (who live out their self-worth issues through their children). Those with Sun in Leo are usually physically strong and make good teachers and role models.

Life Issue: How important am I?

The *Moon in Leo* gives a strong interest in performing of one kind or another. The need for attention from others is very great and most people with this Moon sign will be found in creative fields or having and working with children.

The *Ascendant in Leo* also works at getting attention and recognition, sometimes blatantly so. These types are often found in charge of whatever operations they may be involved with. Very often they are the first son or daughter born in their family, and consequently strive throughout life to recapture their former favorite status.

Ruling Planet: The Sun.

Body: The heart and spine.

Professions: Owning or managing a business. Artistry and musicianship. Acting and directing. Sports. Fashion and entertainment Industry work. Teaching.

Additional Keywords: Style. Warmth. Dramatic impression. Royalty. Gold. Creativity. Performance. The personal touch.

♍ **Virgo** is a sign that is concerned with work, technique, details, and health. People with the Sun in this placement can be detailed, meticulous, practical, clinical, materialistic, critical, and fussy. Virgo is a scientific and intellectual sign, and the desire to classify things is usually present. Work itself is an important issue and there is also a strong service instinct -- Virgo often works for others in a specialized service capacity. The Sun in Virgo suggests a sensitive body which often leads to an interest in healing and diet.

Life Issue: Are things running efficiently?

The *Moon in Virgo* gives an appreciation for competency, cleverness, and craftsmanship. There is usually an interest in medicine or health, or at least associations with the healing professions.

Those with the *Ascendant in Virgo* are usually cautious, careful, and even low-key in social situations. They will rarely, or reluctantly, take a strong lead. They are expert with the details, however, and prosper in helping or consulting professions that require a working knowledge of facts and specifics.

Ruling Planet: Mercury

Body: Intestines

Professions: Service occupations. Secretarial work. Accounting. Legal professions. Health or nutrition-related work. Crafts. Technical work. Electronics.

Additional Keywords: Precision. Details. Low-risk. Sterile. Conservative. Materialistic. High-tech.

♎︎   **Libra,** an air sign, is in many ways the most social of all the signs. The primary motivation for Sun in Libra is human relationships, though this is no guarantee of success in this area. Librans tend to be friendly, considerate, polite, compromising, diplomatic, beauty-conscious, romantic, flirtatious, and sometimes quite lazy. The sign is also sensitive to harmony and balance and requires a calm and peaceful environment to thrive. Decision-making can be a problem, as there is a tendency to look at both sides of an issue very carefully before making any commitment to action.

Life Issue: Let's do it together.

The *Moon in Libra* gives a natural interest in art, music, fashion, and decoration. These are very social people, often very friendly or even flirtatious, who become truly alive only when they are in the company of others. Family is usually an important social outlet for them.

The *Ascendant in Libra* usually produces good-looks, people who dress well and go out of their way to avoid upsets. They are generally eager to please and compromise, at least on the surface. They may also be fond of relaxation and low-energy pursuits.

Ruling Planet: Venus

Body: Kidneys, lower back

Professions: Social work. Counseling. Public relations. Consulting. Designing. Luxury trades. Art.

Additional Keywords: Friendly. Harmonious. Balanced. Decorative. Well-appointed. Soothing. Romantic. Cultured and refined.

♏︎   **Scorpio** is a water sign that attempts to be private, but is generally noticed by everyone. Sun in Scorpio types are serious, determined, secretive, strategic, intense, committed, willful, jealous, and sexual. They may also be dominating and controlling. Scorpio is associated with financial entanglements, sex, birth, and death -- all of which raise survival issues of a material, psychological, or physical nature. This sign has a direct connection to our most primitive instincts, particularly the reproductive urge, the desire for power, and the control of territory. The Sun in Scorpio gives a strong, resilient body and a powerful drive to experience life intensely.

Life Issue: Can I get in any deeper?

The *Moon in Scorpio* gives strong likes and dislikes and an interest in the deeper emotional states of being. This runs from complex relationship entanglements and strong sexual interests to hot, spicy foods. There is also a tendency to repress and control strong feelings that threaten to wreak havoc on daily life.

The *Ascendant in Scorpio* suggests a secretive and strategic social personality. Public information about oneself is usually limited and there is an immediate subconscious awareness of exactly who has what. Scorpio rising is often perceived by others to exude sexuality.

Ruling Planet: Mars and Pluto.

Body: Sexual and eliminative organs.

Professions: The medical fields. Surgery. Therapy. Professions concerned with birthing, aging and dying. Psychology. Corporations. Business. Investments. Financial work. Plumbing. Investigative work. The military. Sanitation.

Additional Keywords: Depth. Dark. Powerful. Primal. Exotic. Sensual. Secretive. Probing. Impressive.

♐ **Sagittarius** is a fire sign that is usually happy, sporty, and often lucky. A driving need with this sign is to experience things firsthand, not just by reading about it. People with the Sun in Sagittarius generally think big and are intuitive, open-minded, playful, and optimistic. There is a tendency to take on more than they can handle. The sign is associated with extending personal experience through broadening activities like travel, sports, publishing, education, and the understanding of life through philosophy and religion. Sun in Sagittarius has such a strong liking for freedom that it often resists agreeing to permanent commitments that threaten restrictions.

Life Issue: How much can I bite off?

The *Moon in Sagittarius* gives an interest in literature, outdoor sports, and travel. These are generous people who are not adverse to taking risks. They have a strong love of freedom and will work to create a lifestyle where they can do what they want.

The *Ascendant in Sagittarius* produces the kind of confident personality that goes with being an entertainer or teacher. The physical build is often tall, or there is an emphasis on the hips and thighs. Walking and running are good exercises for this sign.

Ruling Planet: Jupiter

Body: Hips, thighs, legs, sciatic nerve

Professions: Publishing. Traveling. Writing. Teaching. Law. Religion. Broadcasting. Advertising. Sports.

Additional Keywords: Openness. Expansive, International. Confident. Relaxed. Informal. Sporty. Slapdash. Varied. Educational.

♑ **Capricorn** is an earth sign that has the achievement of social position as its primary motivation. This may be expressed directly, or indirectly by association. People with the Sun in Capricorn are hardworking, practical, traditional, materialistic, reliable, persevering, distant, self-disciplined, organized, scientific, and goal-driven. Being the sign of the father and authority, Capricorn is challenged by issues of responsibility (failure here produces guilt). The sign is quite social and cultured, but conservative and diplomatic; is serious at heart, yet has a sophisticated sense of humor.

Life Issue: Where do I stand relative to others?

The *Moon in Capricorn* gives an interest in business and organization. These are serious people with a need for approval from the public. They have a good business sense and are often successful in the corporate world.

Ascendant in Capricorn produces self-conscious people who are somewhat insecure socially. They often overcompensate for this by taking on responsibilities and management roles. They are generally reliable people who can commit to a project and then deliver it.

Ruling Planet: Saturn

Body: Bones, teeth, joints, knees, hearing.

Professions: Business (executives). Organizing. Accounting. Farming. Teaching (college levels). Mining. Administration. Government.

Additional Keywords: Formality. Tradition. Professional. Restrained. Structured. Heavy. Earthy. Geometric. A purist.

♒︎ **Aquarius** is an air sign that leans toward being unconventional, progressive, inventive, intellectual, different, and sometimes downright weird. People with the Sun in this placement often have strong social motivations and a strong group consciousness, but they don't always fit in with the crowd. Aquarius is about individuality -- but how can you know how individual you are unless you are part of a group? Aquarians are interested in social progress and they are usually liberal-minded and idealistic in these matters. This is an intellectual sign, one that can get fixated on ideas to the point of being inflexible. The Aquarian mind works equally well in both scientific and artistic modes.

Life Issue: Why don't I fit in?

The *Moon in Aquarius* gives an interest in the odd, different, and unusual. Topics that interest these people are well off the mainstream, like astrology, alien visitations, and the sex life of plankton. What's going on in their emotional life may not concern them, however. They have strong freedom needs, like to be a part of a group, and generally have pets.

The *Ascendant in Aquarius* often has socialization problems and tends to go to extremes in their social life. Fitting in well with normal people can be a problem with this rising sign. The commitment to their individuality is strong, but is not always realized without a huge sacrifice.

Ruling Planet: Uranus

Body: Ankles, circulation.

Professions: Social work. The social sciences. Reformer. Inventor. Technical work. Radio. Electronics. Aircraft. Art.

Additional Keywords: Innovation. Unconventional. Technological. Experimental. Deviant. Artistic. Ingenious. Odd. Antique.

♓   **Pisces,** a water sign, is concerned with moving beyond ordinary reality. This is a motivation, or interest, that is generally misunderstood by most other people. People with the Sun in Pisces can be highly sensitive, impressionable, psychic, compassionate, and devoted. At best, Pisces has a deep understanding of the subtleties of art, science, and religion. At worst, it is a confused and escapist sign. Pisces types have a strong serving instinct and a willingness to be self-sacrificing for others, or for a cause. It is the sign of institutions such as hospitals and museums -- places on the edge of society where individuals become less important than "the mission." On the spiritual level, at least, loss of self seems to be a Piscean goal. Belief can make all the difference with this sign. The Sun in Pisces gives a sensitive body and mind and needs a calm environment in which to flourish.

Life Issue: Why am I here?

The *Moon in Pisces* loves the watery world - the sea, lakes, the rain, and the bathtub. Mysteries and irrational pursuits are appealing. There is usually an interest and talent in the arts, especially music, theater, and dance.

The *Ascendant in Pisces* produces a very adaptable personality, but one that is also extremely sensitive to the environment. These types need to be around calm people in calm situations, otherwise they soak up too much negative energy. The sense of self is not very strong with this rising sign and long periods of privacy may be needed to balance out the influences of the world.,

Ruling Planet: Jupiter and Neptune

Body: Feet and lymphatic system.

Professions: Service occupations. Nursing, healing, and hospital work. Secretarial work. Dancing. The arts. Work with liquids (paint, alcohol, water, etc.). Research and development. Religion.

Additional Keywords: Intangible. Escape. Mysterious. Impressionistic. Artistic-bohemian. Chaotic. Spiritual. Soft. The sea. Fish and ships. The color purple. Clouds. Outer space.

Chapter 8:

Houses: Sectors of Sky

The planets in an astrological chart are positioned in both zodiacal signs and within sectors of the sky called houses or domiciles. Signs are a scale for measuring where a planet is located in space which is from the standpoint of the Earth as a whole. Houses are a scale for measuring where a planet is located in its daily cycle created by the rotation of the earth. This is the cycle of rising to setting and then back to rising again. Houses tell where a planet is from the standpoint of a particular spot on Earth. They will reveal if a planet is above or below the horizon, and if it is rising, passing overhead, setting, or passing underfoot on the other side of the Earth.

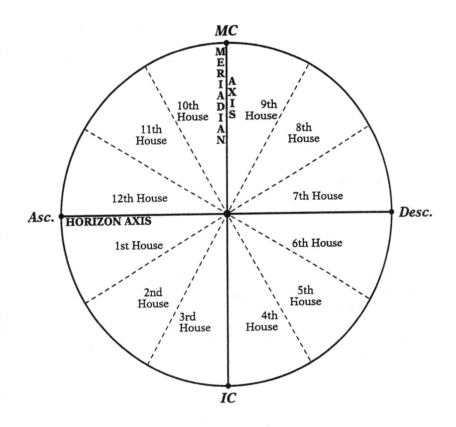

Houses make this local information even more specific by dividing the space surrounding a given point on Earth into twelve sectors. As you can see in the **diagram** on the previous page, the horizon is defined by the axis of the Ascendant-Descendant. At sunrise, the Sun is on the Ascendant, and it enters the twelfth house just after sunrise. About midway between sunrise and noon it would be in the eleventh house; approaching noon it would be in the tenth house; just after noon it would be in the ninth; and so forth, through a 24-hour period until the Sun rises again. The Moon and planets make the same daily progress up in the sky and then down again, each at its own times of day depending on where it happens to be in the zodiac relative to the Sun.

Considering this clockwise daily motion of the planets, you might ask why the houses are numbered counterclockwise. This is probably because ancient astrologers thought of the twelve houses as analogous to the twelve signs. In fact, as we shall see further on, there is some symbolic similarity between the first house and the first sign, the second house and the second sign, etc. Unlike the signs, however, houses can be quite a bit more or less than 30 degrees in length. This is due to geometrical complexities, and it gets more pronounced the further north or south a birth is from the Earth's equator. The exact width of a house also depends on which of the dozens of methods of house division an astrologer uses.

The Ascendant and Midheaven Axes

While there are many ways of dividing the chart into twelve houses, there is no dispute about where the Ascendant and Midheaven (M.C.) are located. These two points, and their opposites, the Descendant and I.C., form the primary divisions of the chart and are the basis for most systems of house division.

The Ascendant is the point where the ecliptic or Sun's path intersects the horizon in the east. At 180 degrees opposite to this, at the other end of the horizon axis, is the Descendant, where the ecliptic intersects the horizon in the west. Planets rise near the Ascendant and set near the Descendant. Taken together, the Ascendant and Descendant form the horizon, or Ascendant axis of the chart. In most methods of house division, these two points mark the cusps of the first and seventh houses. The Ascendant is also known as the Rising Sign.

The Midheaven or M.C. (abbreviation of *medium coeli*, "middle heaven" in Latin) is the point where the Sun's path (ecliptic) intersects the meridian, a great circle in the sky that runs due north and south (directly over the Earth's north and south poles). The M.C. is where the Sun is located at approximately noon; this is the highest any planet can go in its daily cycle when seen from a particular spot on Earth. The I.C. (abbreviated from *imum coeli*, or "lowest heaven") is 180 degrees opposite the M.C.; it is the lowest a planet goes in its daily cycle and where the Sun is located at midnight. The I.C. is actually located on the other side of the Earth from the observer. Together, the M.C. and I.C. form the Midheaven, or meridian, axis of the horoscope. The M.C. and I.C. are usually the cusps of the tenth and fourth houses.

Because the ecliptic, the Sun's path, is tilted about 23 degrees with respect to the Earth's equator, the Ascendant and Midheaven are not always 90 degrees from each other. Rather, their angular relationship changes in the course of the day and is different at different latitudes on Earth. The Ascendant, Descendant, M.C. and I.C. are powerful points in their own right, but they are also the cusps of the first, seventh, tenth, and fourth houses. They also represent the four Cardinal directions (east, west, south, and north) and are called the "angles" of the horoscope. The Gauquelin statistical studies (described in Chapter 1) have provided evidence supporting the importance of these angles -- If a planet is near the Ascendant, M.C., Descendant or I.C., its qualities will tend to manifest strongly in the life of the individual. The Gauquelin studies found that planets near the Ascendant or M.C. tend to be a bit stronger than those near the Descendant or I.C. Astrologers have also found that planets in aspect to one of these points tend to assume importance in the chart, particularly the hard 90-degree, 45-degree, and 135-degree aspects. Along with the Sun and Moon, the Ascendant and M.C. are the most important points in the horoscope.

House Systems

The Ascendant-Descendant axis divides the chart into upper and lower hemispheres, so that planets are defined as being either above the horizon or below it. The M.C.-I.C. axis divides the chart into eastern and western hemispheres, with planets that are on their way up and those that are on their way down. These four angles of the horoscope divide the chart into four quadrants. Further division of these quadrants into three sections each is the basis for most of the numerous methods of house division. (A few methods use only the Ascendant or

M.C. as reference points.) In general, however, with only slight differences, all house systems measure where the planets are in their daily cycle around the Earth.

The beginnings or "cusps" of the first, fourth, seventh and tenth houses are not usually a matter of dispute because they coincide with the angles (Ascendant, Descendant, M.C., I.C.). Most astrologers take these cusps quite seriously if they are sure the birth time is reasonably accurate. The cusps of the other houses (two, three, five, six, eight, nine, eleven, and twelve) can be different depending on the house method used. Many astrologers regard these intermediate house cusps as only approximate; a planet near the end of one house is thought by many astrologers to partake somewhat of the qualities of the next house. Today, most English-speaking astrologers use the Placidus or Koch house systems; others use equal (30-degree) houses starting at the Ascendant. In Europe you might hear more about Regiomontanus houses; siderealists use Campanus houses; and in India, Porphyry houses are used. Dozens of methods of house division exist: this is one area in astrology on which there has never been much agreement.

What the Houses Show

Whereas the fastest-moving planetary body, the Moon, takes a month to go around the zodiac, the houses take only 24 hours to make one cycle. The houses are thus the fastest-moving part of the horoscope. The degree of the zodiac that marks the beginning of a house advances on the average of one degree for every four minutes of time. Therefore, to erect an astrological chart with accurate houses, we need to know the exact time of day that a person was born. Also, the houses represent how the heavens look from a particular spot on Earth. Two people born at the same time may have planets in the same degrees of the zodiac, but, unless they are born very close to each other geographically, their Ascendant, Midheaven, and intermediate house cusps will be different. This is the reason astrologers need also to know the latitude and longitude at which a person was born.

Time and geographical variables make houses an element of the horoscope that best describe an individual's particular circumstances in life. Two people born on the same day but at different times may have the same underlying urges, as shown by the relationships of the planets in the zodiac. But the way these urges find their outlet in daily life is shown by the houses which can be dramatically different in the charts of births separated by just a few minutes.

The house in which a planet is located shows the area of life in which its influence is most likely to manifest. In astrological interpretation, the houses are used to determine the kinds of experiences that are most natural, appropriate, and likely to occur for the individual in each of the various areas of the life. Also, the sign on the beginning or cusp of a house indicates to the astrologer how the area of life associated with that house will tend to operate.

Meanings of the Houses

The *first* house extends from the Ascendant (the cusp of the first house) to about thirty degrees below the horizon. The Ascendant point itself symbolizes the mask, persona, or presentation of self in the social world. Like the Ascendant, the first house also has much to do with the social identity and personality. Traditionally, it is said to define the natural self-expression, the physical body and appearance, mannerisms, temperament, and social attitudes. It also symbolizes self-awareness and the assertion of self.

The *second* house symbolizes the abilities we have that are worth something in a practical sense. It shows our resources, ownership, money, possessions, talents and skills.

The *third* house traditionally rules communication, correspondence, neighbors, siblings, relatives, local mobility, and the local environment. It has to do with both the nature of our immediate environment, social and physical, and how we might best come to terms with it.

The *fourth* house rules the domestic home, the base of operations, parents, family, the ancestral tradition or roots, property, and internal personal security. It symbolizes the very personal and emotional experience of centering and securing oneself in the world.

The *fifth* house is the area of self-enhancement, usually expressed through children, artistic creativity, or game-playing. This house rules salesmanship, "show business," love affairs, and courtship -- all a kind of performance.

The *sixth* house is about work, crises, and adjustments, and it is says much about the daily routine and schedule. The mastery of specific techniques and service to others are also themes. It is also the house of mental and physical health -- our ability to make things (including the body) run smoothly and efficiently.

The *seventh* house signifies marriage, business partnerships, and other one-to-one relationships. It has to do with awareness of others in general and with the ability to participate and cooperate. It also indicates open enemies, those with whom we openly compete.

The *eighth* house is the area of shared resources, of materials that are jointly owned or are used with other people. It covers inheritances and trusts, and any other type of financial entanglement. It is associated with shared rituals, including reunions, which function to revitalize relationships. The basic issue here is trust, a necessary ingredient in sexual matters and in sustaining relationships. The 8th house is the house of divorce, crisis, mystery, occultism, and death and the beyond.

The *ninth* house provides information about the search for meaning in life. It is associated with travel, education, religion, higher knowledge, philosophy, law, and deep mental comprehension. Promotion, publishing, and advertising, which involve extending ideas to many minds, all come under its rule.

The *tenth* house usually begins at the Midheaven, which, like the Ascendant, is in itself a very important personal point in the birthchart. The tenth house has to do with life direction and career. It shows our vocation or calling in life, our reputation and status. It is our public persona and shows how we fit into our community. Like the fourth house, the tenth house is also associated with parents.

The *eleventh* house rules friends, groups, associations, and organizations. It symbolizes our activities within social units, our social aspirations, and the values held by our friends and peers.

The *twelfth* house rules personal spiritual crises. It is the area of hidden and secret things, psychic experiences, illumination, personal sacrifice, karma, solitude, and confinement. It symbolizes powers greater than the self, such as institutions and belief systems. Confinement is often the result of failing to conform to the rules or rituals of institutions or belief systems. The twelfth house is also the house of failures and defeats and how we deal with them.

A Personal Zodiac

As mentioned above, the houses are a 12-fold cycle tied to a particular point on earth, rather than to a point in the heavens, the way the signs are. Houses are thought of as kind of personal zodiac, somewhat parallel to the signs in meaning. For example, connections can be made between the first house and the first sign, Aries. People with many planets in the first house may be very self-absorbed, as are those with many planets in Aries. Many fashion models have Venus in the first house, their physical appearance being the most important element in their lives. Planets in the second house are, like planets in Taurus, related to money and resources. The third house, like Gemini, involves learning, talking, and visiting neighbors. In the fourth house, as in Cancer, emotional matters, home, family, nesting, and nurturing are major themes. Leo corresponds to the fifth house, which has to do with performance and creativity. People often have children when major planets transit the fifth house. The sixth house has to do with work, health, schedules, etc., much like Virgo.

The next six houses follow the same pattern. The seventh house is, like Libra, associated with relationships, particularly partnerships and marriages. The eighth house is like Scorpio in that the issues are sex, death, trust, and sharing. The ninth house, which indicates travel, learning and legal matters, can be linked to Sagittarius. Capricorn and the tenth house rule honor, status and reputation. Aquarius and the eleventh house show friends, groups, and other social associations. Pisces and the twelfth house are both linked with the unfinished, the complex and the unseen.

While they share some common themes, houses and signs serve different functions in the chart. Houses show the particular departments of life in which a planet is likely to have its strongest influence. Signs, on the other hand, are more like adjectives that further color or qualify the planets and houses. Houses show *where* (in life) the planets operate; signs show *how* they express.

The Planets in the Houses

Each planet has its own particular effect on the matters indicated by the house in which it is located. Many planets in a house indicate an emphasis on the matters of that house; more than one trend may be discernible. The natural trend of a house's particular area of life is also symbolized by the zodiacal sign on the house cusp, especially when there are no planets in that house.

The *Sun* gives great emphasis to the house where it is located. There will be a need to center the life around that house's issues, and those issues will be strong and well-defined. For example, with the Sun in the third house, there would be a need to focus on relatives, siblings, neighbors and matters of communication and transportation.

The *Moon* suggests that matters of the house it falls in are likely to be reactive, affected by emotions and moods, and characterized by fluctuations and frequent changes.

Mercury gives a pronounced mental or communicative tendency to the matters of its house. Such matters are usually handled rationally.

Venus emphasizes the emotional aspects of the area of life indicated by its house position. Venus stimulates the desire nature, but generally brings positive results.

Mars suggests activity and construction. It symbolizes both strife and a need to take initiative in the matters ruled by the house in which it is located.

Jupiter brings optimism, balance, growth and luck, usually making its house a noticeably successful area of life.

The house position of *Saturn* indicates the matters that need to be approached consciously and logically. These matters can be prone to delays and problems, which require patience, discipline, and organization to solve them.

Uranus tends to disrupt the matters of its house position, and suggests erratic and unstable patterns and a need for spontaneity and experimentation.

Neptune suggests blind spots and a tendency to dwell on ideals or the future. The areas of life indicated by its house position need to be handled intuitively, creatively, and sensitively.

Pluto often subjects its house's matters to shocks and deep transformations. Pluto intensifies things and suggests the need for changes and new beginnings.

The Horoscope

Having outlined planets, aspects, signs and houses, we are now ready to show how they all interact in a horoscope. Most astrologers in the West read from horoscopes that are circular in form somewhat like that shown below.

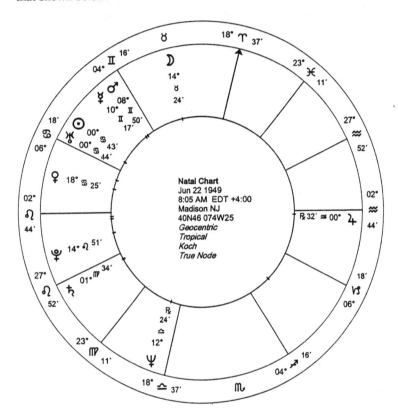

In the horoscope, the houses are noted by sign, degree, and minute. In the chart depicted here, the Ascendant, or cusp of the first house, is 2 degrees 44 minutes of Leo (2♌44). Each planet is located in a house and is indicated by its symbol or glyph, along with the degrees and minutes of its sign position. The resulting diagram or map of the sky, the horoscope wheel, gives us the main information we need to interpret the chart. As you can see here, the Sun is near the cusp of the twelfth house; the person was born a little over two hours after sunrise. This is the horoscope of Meryl Streep.

Relocating the Houses: Astro-Mapping

A birth occurs at a specific instant in time -- but where this birth occurs on the globe can make a difference. A birth occurring at 9 AM in New York would be at a time when the Sun was well up into the sky, probably in the 11th house of the birth chart for this moment. At this same instant, however, the Sun was just rising in Los Angeles, probably in the 1st house of the chart calculated for that location. In Hawaii at this instant, the Sun had not yet risen and wouldn't for several hours.

Astrologers have found that when people move away from their birth place, they become sensitive to a chart of their instant of birth at their new location. The zodiacal positions of the planets in the new (relocated) chart remain the same as the birth chart, but the house positions change, and this factor can alter the planetary emphasis. Exactly where on earth these planetary shifts occur can be plotted on a map. The use of these maps can give an interesting perspective on the potential effects of a relocation. This technique is called astro-mapping or astro-cartography.

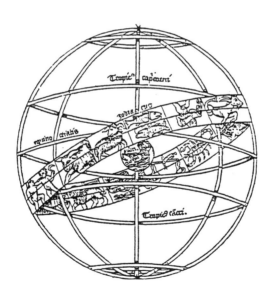

Chapter 9:

Reading a Birth Chart

The art of interpreting a birth chart requires a thorough knowledge of astrological symbols, extensive experience, and good judgment. Teaching this skill is well beyond the scope of this book. Still, anyone with some patience, common sense, and the ability to add can extract some valuable and accurate information from a chart. To give you an introductory idea of how an astrological interpretation proceeds, here are some specific suggestions and guidelines for reading a birthchart. As an illustration, we will use the example chart on the next page.

Steps in Evaluating a Chart

*Look for **Angular Planets***

The first thing to look for is a conjunction of any planet with the angles of the horoscope; the Ascendant, M.C., Descendant, or I.C. As we said before, angular planets tend to be far more powerful than planets located elsewhere. In fact, planets within 10 degrees of an angle are usually the most powerful planets in the chart. Such prominence of any planet(s) suggests much about how the person experiences life and interacts with others. For example, when Saturn is angular, the personality tends to be security conscious; when Mars is angular, the personality tends to be aggressive. It is this type of effect which has been proven statistically by the Gauquelins. In the example chart on the next page, Mercury is within 9 degrees of the M.C.

*Tally Up the **Elements and Qualities***

The next step is to measure the relative distribution of planets by Element. This can be done with a weighted scoring system in which the outer planets (Jupiter, Saturn, Uranus, Neptune, and Pluto) are worth one point each, the inner planets (Mercury, Venus and Mars) are worth two points each, and the Sun, Moon, and Ascendant are worth three points each. Angular planets (those located within five degrees of the Ascendant, M.C., Descendant, and I.C.) also receive a score of three points. Using the example chart, one should arrive at the following scores:

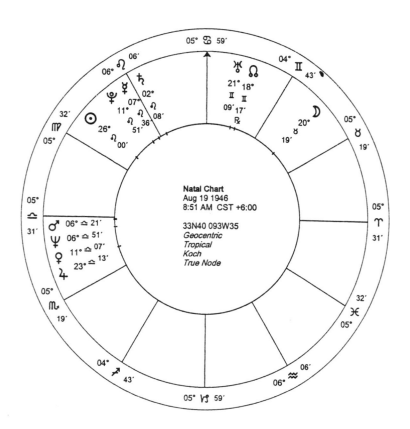

Example chart: **August 19, 1946, 8:51 AM CST,
somewhere in Arkansas.**

Fire signs: Saturn (1) + Mercury (2) + Pluto (1) + Sun (3) = 6 points
Earth signs: Moon (3) = 3 points
Air signs: Uranus (1) + Ascendant (3) + Mars, angular (3)
+ Neptune, angular (3) + Venus (2) + Jupiter (1) = 13 points
Water signs: no planets = 0 points

Next, using the same scoring system, determine the relative emphasis
of the Qualities.

Cardinal signs: Ascendant (3) + Mars, angular (3)
+ Neptune angular (3) + Venus (2) + Jupiter (1) = 12 points

Fixed signs: Moon (3) + Saturn (1) + Mercury (2)
+ Pluto (1) + Sun (3) = 10 points

Mutable signs: Uranus (1) = 1 point

In this example horoscope, one can immediately see that the element Air and the quality Cardinal prevail. The individual would tend to have the qualities of Air signs prominent in the personality. These are curiosity, an active mind, and a need for communication. Cardinal qualities would symbolize a tendency toward initiatives, action, and outreach. This is a person who doesn't hesitate to make connections with others.

Tally the *Hemisphere Emphasis*

The next step is to determine the hemisphere emphasis, if any. Using the same scoring system (except for the extra value placed on angular planets), compute the relative weight of the planets *above* the horizon (in houses 7 through 12) versus those *below* (in houses 1 through 6). Naturally, the Ascendant is not used here. Planets above the horizon, or in the upper hemisphere, signify an emphasis on the public and community life. Planets below the horizon, or in the lower hemisphere, signify inner and family life.

Planets above the horizon: Moon (3) + Uranus (1)
+ Saturn (1) + Mercury (2) + Pluto (1) + Sun (3)   = 11 points

Planets below the horizon: Mars (2) + Neptune (2)
+ Venus (2) + Jupiter (1)   = 7 points

In this case, the above-the-horizon score is higher. This suggests that the person would tend to live a public life, as opposed to a more private one characteristic of those with a high score of below-the-horizon. This person would be more concerned with consensus reality (what other people think is true) than with their own internal reality.

Next, determine the relative scores for planets in the *eastern hemisphere* (houses 10 through 3) versus those in the *western hemisphere* (houses 4 through 9). The eastern hemisphere, where the planets are rising, suggests drive and self-directedness. The western hemisphere, where planets are setting, suggests cooperation or reliance on others.

Planets in the east: Saturn (1) + Mercury (2) + Jupiter (1) + Sun (3)
+ Pluto (1) + Mars (2) + Neptune (1) + Venus (2)   = 13 points

Planets in the west: Moon (3) + Uranus (1)   = 4 points

With a higher score for planets in the east, this person is likely to show initiative and leadership qualities. This is a person who pulls himself up by the bootstraps.

Having thus organized the information in the chart, you can answer basic questions about the person as shown in the outline below. This same information could also be obtained through a lengthy psychological questionnaire or interview, but, as many psychologists are beginning to realize, astrology can give it more quickly and without the development of a personal relationship.

An Astrological Personality Profile

1.*Self/Other Directed.* Is the person self-directed, independent and capable of taking action alone? Indications are:
> a. Fire-sign emphasis.
> b. Majority of planets in the east.
> c. Sun, Mars, or Uranus angular.
> d. Sun or Moon conjunct Mars.

Or is the person other-directed, one who responds and is cooperative with others? Indications are:
> a. Majority of planets in the west.
> b. Sun, Moon, or many planets in the sign Libra or Pisces.
> c. Venus or Moon angular.

2. *Thinker/Feeler.* Is the person predominantly left-brained, a thinker and analyzer of things who tends to rationalize and find logical solutions to problems? Indications are:
> a. Air-sign emphasis.
> b. Mercury, Saturn, or Uranus angular.
> c. Moon in an Air sign or in conjunction with Mercury, Saturn, or Uranus.

Or is the person predominantly right-brained, one who feels and knows intuitively what to do? Indications are:
> a. Water-sign emphasis.
> b. Moon or Neptune angular.
> c. Sun or Ascendant in conjunction the Moon or Neptune.

3. *Idealistic/Practical.* Does the person tend to look at life in terms of potential? Indications are:
> a. Air-sign or Fire-sign emphasis.
> b. Sun, Moon, or Ascendant in an Air sign.
> c. Mutable-sign emphasis.
> d. Neptune angular or conjunct Sun or Moon.

Or does the person tend to value what is practical and at hand?
Indications are:

    a. Earth-sign or Water-sign emphasis.

    b. Sun, Moon, or Ascendant in an Earth sign.

    c. Sun, Moon, or Ascendant in conjunction with Saturn.

    d. Saturn angular.

4. *Emotional Control/Expressivity.* Does the person control emotions like excitement and anger? Indications are:

    a. Moon, Venus, or Ascendant in Air or Earth signs.

    b. Moon or Venus in conjunction with Saturn or Uranus.

    c. Fixed-sign emphasis.

Or express emotions openly and directly? Indications are:

    a. Moon, Venus, or Ascendant in Fire signs.

    b. Moon and Venus in conjunction with Mars, Jupiter
       or Neptune.

    c. Water-sign emphasis in the chart.

5. *Strong/Weak Sexual Drives.* Does the person have strong sexual motivations? Indications are:

    a. Mars in conjunction with Venus, Moon, or Pluto.

    b. Sun, Moon, Mars, or Venus in Taurus or Scorpio.

    c. Pluto angular.

Or low sexual drives, having the sex drive redirected elsewhere?
Indications are:

    a. Venus or Mars in conjunction with Saturn.

    b. Moon, Venus, or Mars in Air signs or in Virgo
       or Capricorn.

6. *Flexibility/Rigidity.* Is the person flexible and adaptable?
Indications are:

    a. Mutable-sign emphasis.

    b. Sun, Moon, or Ascendant in a Mutable sign.

    c. Mercury or Venus angular.

Or rigid and resistant to change? Indications are:

    a. Fixed-sign emphasis.

    b. Sun, Moon, or Ascendant in a Fixed sign.

    c. Sun, Saturn, or Uranus angular.

7. *Socially Active/Private.* Does the person prefer to be social and active in community matters? Indications are:

    a. Majority of planets above the horizon.

    b. Air or Fire sign emphasis.

    c. Sun, Mercury, Mars, or Jupiter angular.

Or does the person prefer to be private and close to the home and family? Indications are:

    a. Majority of planets below the horizon.

    b. Water-sign or Earth-sign emphasis.

    c. Saturn, Neptune, or Pluto angular.

Applying these considerations to the example chart, we can learn that:

1. The person is probably self-directed because most of the planets are located in the east and Mars is angular.
2. The person is mentally active and an analyzer because the majority of planets and the Ascendant are in Air signs.
3. The person tends to be an idealist due to the high score in Air signs, including the Ascendant, and an angular Neptune.
4. The person tends to both express feeling and control his or her feelings because the Ascendant and Venus are in an Air sign but Venus is in conjunction with Mars and Neptune.
5. This person's sex drive is probably high because Mars is in conjunction with Venus and the Moon is in Taurus.
6. With the Sun and Moon in Fixed signs, but with Venus angular, this person is only moderately resistant to change.
7. This person is socially active because the majority of planets are above the horizon, in Air or Fire signs, with Mars and Jupiter angular.

The chart we have just analyzed is that of President Bill Clinton.

Astrology and Self-Knowledge

To be successful as individuals, we need to understand our own nature and how we interact with others. There are a number of routes to self-knowledge, including psychology, religion, and just plain common sense. Astrology is an excellent path toward self-understanding and it can offer much more to the seeker than conventional routes, although it is generally not placed in that category due to prejudice. In fact, astrology provides a coherent structure to the viewpoints provided by psychology, philosophy, religion, and most self-help books. Of the numerous models that attempt to explain the human situation, astrology is the most inclusive.

Psychologists have observed that what we call personality is really a composite of several sub-personalities or themes. Over the past 100 years, psychologists have proposed a number of personality models that attempt to account for what might be called the plurality of the self. There is Freud's id, ego, and superego, and Jung's extrovert-introvert polarity and his four functions. Sheldon delineated three basic somatypes, personalities based on body shape. Transactional analysis talks of the critical parent, the rebellious child, and the free child. None of these models can even begin to approach what astrology has to offer. The astrological chart is a stunning model of the self, its plurality, and its projections -- and it's not just one psychologist's idea. An understanding of just the Sun, Moon, and Ascendant signs alone equals or surpasses anything that psychology has produced so far. The most simplistic use of astrology can open up whole new vistas in self-understanding. Adding to this the other planets and the aspects opens the door to an even more expansive perspective.

The astrological chart shows the true nature of the self, and the lines of least resistance in the development of personality. Culture, society, and family have a powerful influence on individuals, shaping them in conformity with one tradition or another. Some people spend most of their lives fighting these forces, and they can become mentally and physically ill in doing so. Astrology offers a way of defining and acknowledging who we are, and of knowing who we are not.

Take as an example a man with the Sun in Pisces, who was born into a business-oriented family and, even with a string of successful business deals to his credit, felt somehow unfulfilled. Learning about the symbolism and needs of the sign Pisces led him to try his hand at art and eventually he became a successful studio model painter. Without input from astrology, this might never have occurred to him because there had been no precedent for such activities in his family.

The Sun in the birthchart symbolizes the primary motivations in life, the activities and directions that give meaning to life. We should learn to follow our Sun-sign motivations, because they are ultimately central to our growth. A lifestyle built around our Sun-sign is empowering, vitalizing, and offers the best possibilities for over-all integration of the self. While the Sun symbolizes who we really are, the Moon shows our interests, what we need to feed on. The Ascendant shows our social personality, the roles we play, how we come across to others, and how we mix with our friends, partners and family.

Self-knowledge is the first step toward wisdom. Knowing ourselves, we are masters of our destiny. Although a complete astrological perspective can only be provided through a reading of the birthchart in its entirety, a simple knowledge of Sun, Moon, and Ascendant signs can provide a foundation for a better understanding of our true nature.

Fate and Free-Will

Earlier in this guide the fate/free-will problem was discussed in the context of twins. The perspective of this author is that we are fated in several ways. First, we are fated, or restricted, by our physical, emotional and mental predispositions. None of us can fly like birds. Most of us will never become major league basketball players or leading rocket scientists, no matter how hard we try. But we may be able to excel in a field appropriate to our chart. Astrology tells us who we are. Fate is limits, and all of us have them. By knowing our limitations, we cease to be victims -- we learn how to work with our limits or how to extend capabilities.

Second, we are fated in the sense that our birthchart is ours for life and that when one of its cycles (planetary configurations) becomes active, we need to respond in some way. This is a kind of fate in the context of time. Our free-will lies in the quality of our responses to these needs. As we become more aware and conscious of who we are, we become capable of making more intelligent decisions and choices. Every choice we have to make is thus an opportunity to exercise our free-will. It is ignorance about who we are that keeps us fated.

Astrology and Mythology

There is another, deeper way of using astrology to understand ourselves that lies in an understanding of mythology. Myths are stories about typical instinctual patterns and responses in the culture at large. They describe basic (archetypal) themes central to human life and destiny. Many of the Greco-Roman myths are dramas that explain the interweaving of archetypal themes by depicting the interactions of gods and goddesses. We can look at planets (which were named for the gods) as personifications of the human urges and destiny patterns in the myths. By doing this and looking at constellations in which planets or sensitive points are located, we can read the birthchart as a stage on which stories unfold. The strongest planets and the most dominant constellations in the chart are indicators pointing to the most relevant myths for that person.

As we know, if a planet is in conjunction or close aspect with the Sun, Moon, or the angles of a birthchart, its influence over one's life is very significant and its general nature will be noticeable in many ways. For example, take a person whose Sun is conjunct Mars. This suggests an urge towards power and taking initiative. But it can also be looked upon as a signature of the warrior-hero. Such an individual may benefit from an understanding of warrior-hero myths because these will describe his most basic inclinations, and consequently, his destiny. From this perspective, the birthchart is a composite of destiny themes that give structure and meaning to existence.

Relationships

In the final analysis, the quality of our lives is based on the quality of our relationships. We simply cannot ignore human relationships, and any subject that provides reliable information about them should be considered valuable. Astrology offers several techniques by which relationships can be understood and evaluated. One technique, called synastry, involves comparing the planetary positions of one chart to those of another. Although the comparison of two birthcharts can become quite technical and complex, there are a few general rules that anyone can apply when judging potential compatibility.

Rule #1. A sign is compatible with other signs of the same Element. Also, Fire mixes well with Air, and Earth combines well with Water. For example, Aries is a Fire sign and will therefore be compatible with the other Fire signs, Leo and Sagittarius. Aries will also be compatible with the Air signs, Gemini, Libra, and Aquarius. Similarly, Earth signs will be compatible with each other and with Water signs. See the table below for compatibilities.

Fire signs: Aries, Leo, Sagittarius
Air signs: Gemini, Libra, Aquarius
Earth signs: Taurus, Virgo, Capricorn
Water signs: Cancer, Scorpio, Pisces

Rule #2. Compatibility between signs that are opposite each other can vary. In some cases relationships between persons of opposite signs may become stressful because of differences. In other cases, they complement each other well. Below is a listing of the opposite signs.

Aries - Libra   Cancer - Capricorn   Taurus - Scorpio
Leo - Aquarius   Gemini - Sagittarius   Virgo - Pisces

Rule #3. Compare symbols which are similar. Examples: Sun to Sun, Moon to Moon, Ascendant to Ascendant, Venus to Venus, etc.

Compatibility of Sun-signs is important for long-term relationships. Because the Sun sign indicates the basic motivations and goals in life, incompatibility here may produce stress, avoidance, and the possible domination/submission of one individual to the other.

Moon-sign compatibility is important where living together is concerned. Moon-sign compatibility indicates that the general interests, emotions, moods, and eating and sleeping habits will not conflict seriously.

Ascendant compatibility is important where two people must make a good showing together in front of others. Ascendant compatibility also indicates that two people will appreciate the general appearance of each other.

Venus compatibility is important in intimate relationships because it symbolizes the way a person loves and what they value in love. People with their Venus positions in compatible signs will understand each other's loving style easily.

Rule #4. Note the relationship between the Sun of one person and the Moon of the other. Also note any interconnections between the Moon of one and the Ascendant and Midheaven of the other. Relationships are likely to prosper where the Sun sign of one person relates favorably with the other person's Moon sign. This is also true when the Moon of one partner is in conjunction with the Ascendant, M.C., Descendant, or I.C. of the other.

Synastry, the Composite Chart, and the Relationship Chart

The judgment of the planetary contacts between two charts is called *synastry.* While the preceding section might serve as a foundation to this topic, the serious study of synastry can become quite complex and requires mastery of several astrological techniques. It is possible through synastry to judge a number of things about a relationship including major partnership issues, sexual attraction, communication potential, and relative dominance.

The *composite* chart is also used in evaluating a relationships; this is a chart that is derived by combining two natal charts. To create a composite chart, the zodiacal midpoints of each matched pair of planets and houses must be computed. For example, if one person has the Moon at 5 degrees of Aries and the other has the Moon at 5 degrees of Leo, then the composite Moon would be at 5 degrees of Gemini, half-way between the two. The composite chart shows how the relationship functions as an entity in itself and is often used in evaluating established relationships like marriages and business partnerships. Composite charts can also be constructed for three or more persons and are useful in evaluating group dynamics.

The *relationship chart* is a chart calculated for the midpoint in time and space between two births. Here's an example. One person was born on December 21st, 1965 in New York City. Another was born on June 21st, 1966 in Los Angeles. The midpoint in time between their births was March 21st, 1966, and the midpoint in space was in Kansas. Their relationship chart would then be a chart calculated for March 21st, 1966 in Kansas. Like the composite chart, this chart is descriptive of how the two individuals blend.

Chapter 10:

Choosing the Best Time to Take Action

The Phases of the Moon

Many calendars carry on an old tradition -- they show the four phases of the Moon each month. This tradition dates back to the times when the livelihoods of farmers and seafarers depended on such information. The four phases of the Moon are: the new Moon (when the Moon is conjunct the Sun); the first quarter, when the Moon is in a square aspect with the Sun; the full Moon, when it moves opposite the Sun; and the third quarter, when it is once again square the Sun and on its way back toward the new Moon phase.

For centuries, men and women have planned their activities around this Sun-Moon cycle. It indicates when things will grow, what the weather might be, and when an action taken would get good results. Much of this knowledge has been lost during the past few centuries as our civilization has moved farther away from a connection with nature. We still know a few things about the Moon, however. We know that the highest tides occur at full and new Moon, and that the behavior of people in "mental institutions" can be intense around the full Moon. There are often heavy rains, and the stock market fluctuates noticeably, about three to five days after new and full Moons. The following are a few general rules about the Moon that have proven their worth over time.

1. Start important new activities (such as opening a business, planting a garden, getting married, building a house, etc.) between the new Moon and the full Moon (the first half of the cycle). The closer to the full Moon, the more rapidly the activity will proceed. Move to finish up incomplete projects, or start secret or hidden projects, between the full and new Moon (the second half of the cycle).

2. Do not start important activities on the exact day of the new or full Moon, or within a day of the quarter Moon. Activities started at the quarter are likely to develop major problems.

3. Make important decisions at the full Moon. The full Moon is a time for clarification in relationships and for deep understanding.

Using Lunar Aspects

The Moon takes just over two days to travel (transit) through a sign. During this time it forms aspects with the other planets, some favorable, some stressful. There are many astrological calendars and ephemerides which list these lunar aspects, some even giving the exact time of day that each aspect occurs and also the time that the Moon is "void-of-course" (see below).

In general, when choosing a date to do something, like traveling or opening a business, it is better to choose a day when the Moon forms positive aspects (trines and sextiles) to the other planets. The one day each month when the Moon is conjunct Jupiter is usually a good day to start a project. Conversely, it may be best to avoid beginning important projects on days when the Moon forms many adverse aspects (squares and oppositions) with the other planets, particularly with Saturn.

The Void-of-Course Moon

After the Moon has completed making all its aspects with the other planets, it must finish its transit through the sign that it is in. This period of time, which begins when the last lunar aspect occurs and finishes when the Moon enters the next sign, is the time when the Moon is void-of-course. This period can last anywhere from a few minutes to a day or more, depending on where the other planets happen to be located. Traditionally, only the Ptolemaic aspects (the conjunction, sextile, square, trine, and opposition) are used in determining whether or not the Moon is void-of-course.

When the Moon is void-of-course, it is best not to begin new projects or take unnecessary risks. More often than not, projects initiated under a void-of-course Moon will go nowhere or end up requiring major adjustments and refinishing. The time that the Moon is void-of-course is not a time for action, but rather a time for quiet and meditation. It is also good for catching up on unfinished business, reviewing, rearranging things, and for simply letting things happen. Listings of when the Moon is void-of-course can be found in many ephemerides and astrological calendars.

The Angularity of Jupiter, Sun and Venus

As we know, planets which are rising, setting, culminating, and anti-culminating (at lower culmination) are more powerful than when they are in other positions. In the same way, events which are started when a planet occupies one of these powerful positions tend to be strongly influenced by that planet. It is best to start projects or take risks when Jupiter, the Sun, or Venus (the traditionally beneficial planets) are near the Ascendant, M.C., Descendant, or I.C. Conversely, one would not want to take risks when Saturn is angular. But if you wanted to do something formal, or something that was to endure, then Saturn would be an appropriate significator. As a general rule, determine the planet that best signifies what you want to do, then do it when that planet is angular and therefore at an energy peak in its daily (diurnal) cycle. There are four times each day when a planet is near an angle. These times can be determined from *Valliere's Natural Cycles Almanac*, a yearly publication that offers graphs for each month like the one shown below.

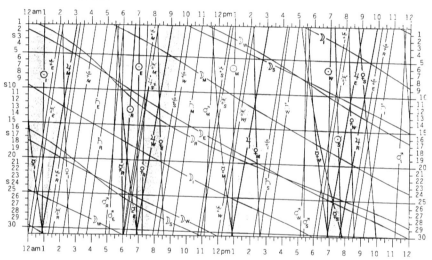

R=rising, M=upper meridian, S=setting, I=lower meridian

Ma	I	2.25	0h10m	11:36 AM	Ur	S	200.01	13h20m	0:48 AM
Ne	I	10.13	0h41m	12:07 PM	Me	S	209.45	13h59m	1:27 AM
Su	R	12.09	0h49m	12:15 PM	Su	S	229.17	15h17m	2:45 AM
Mo	S	13.49	0h55m	12:21 PM	Mo	R	239.14	15h57m	3:25 AM
Pl	R	27.01	1h48m	1:14 PM	Sa	S	248.40	16h35m	4:02 AM
Sa	R	41.58	2h48m	2:14 PM	Pl	S	250.36	16h42m	4:10 AM
Ju	I	79.15	5h17m	4:42 PM	Ju	M	259.15	17h17m	4:44 AM
Ve	M	84.54	5h40m	5:05 PM	Ve	I	264.54	17h40m	5:07 AM
Ur	M	88.07	5h52m	5:18 PM	Ur	I	268.07	17h52m	5:20 AM
Ma	R	93.01	6h12m	5:37 PM	Ma	S	271.50	18h07m	5:35 AM
Me	M	99.51	6h39m	6:05 PM	Ne	S	277.53	18h32m	5:59 AM
Ne	R	102.33	6h50m	6:15 PM	Me	I	279.51	18h39m	6:07 AM
Su	M	120.43	8h03m	7:28 PM	Su	I	300.43	20h03m	7:30 AM
Mo	I	126.32	8h26m	7:51 PM	Mo	M	306.32	20h26m	7:53 AM

Angularity of planets as a list

The times that planets are on the angles can also be found by using a computer program. On the facing page is the output from Barry Orr's *Astrologers Planetarium* program. Here you see the dates and time for a particular locality when a planet is rising, culminating, setting, or at lower culmination.

Mercury Retrograde

There is a planetary phenomenon that occurs three times per year that is very obvious to anyone who cares to pay attention to it. These are the periods when Mercury is retrograde. Paying attention to this phenomenon could save time and trouble, and make life easier and more comprehensible for many people. As Mercury orbits the Sun, it never actually retrogrades or goes backward, but it appears to do so from our vantage point on Earth. As seen from the Earth, there is the following sequence of events:

1. Mercury speeds through four consecutive signs of the zodiac. Faster than any planet, its speed is exceeded only by that of the Moon.

2. Mercury then slows down and stops. This is called Mercury's *first station*. Where this turning point occurs with respect to your birthchart is very important for you.

3. For about three weeks, Mercury appears to move in a reverse direction, then slows down and stops for a second time. This is its *retrograde* movement and its *second station*. Again, where this station occurs in your chart is important.

4. Once more moving in its natural, "forward" direction, Mercury gradually gains speed. About six weeks after step #2 began, Mercury passes the point where it made its first station. This is sometimes referred to as Mercury passing out of its *shadow*. The sequence of events is now complete, and Mercury moves ahead at top speed again for the next three months.

The part of your birthchart where Mercury makes its retrograde loop becomes activated in several ways. First, there is an emphasis on matters signified by the house in which Mercury goes retrograde. For example, Mercury retrograde in your seventh house would turn up the volume on relationships, particularly partnerships such as marriage. Second, if you were to initiate new, untried activities at this time, matters associated with this house would begin to become more complex and difficult to manage. For example, if you got married (for the first time) while Mercury was retrograding in your seventh house, you might have some serious problems with this marriage. But Mercury retrograde in the seventh house could indicate a favorable time to re-marry. This is the secret of using Mercury retrograde to your advantage: While it's retrograde, do things you've already done before. The matters emphasized by the Mercury retrograde begin to return to normal around the time that Mercury passes its first station.

On a more general level, the sign in which Mercury retrogrades can provide useful information. Mercury retrograde in (or opposite) your Sun sign often indicates problems like paperwork overload, transportation complications, delays, and a general lack of progress -- but it could also be a time when you catch up with unfinished business.

Those born with the Sun in Gemini or Virgo seem to suffer the most during the times when Mercury is retrograde, since both signs are said to be ruled by Mercury. This is also true of those born with Gemini or Virgo Ascendants. Astrologers have noticed that an unusual number of persons born under these signs experience stress on the very days that Mercury makes a station. Most frequently, problems have to do with transportation and communication.

It is also true that those houses in a birthchart with Gemini and Virgo on the cusps are affected by this erratic planet. Those with Virgo on the cusp of the second house (ruling money and purchases) should probably not buy anything new by mail-order when Mercury is retrograde, but it would be appropriate to purchase items that either complete an earlier purchase or require completion later on, and these are likely to proceed without problems.

On a worldly level, the stations of Mercury almost always coincide with major news events, often those involving transportation. It seems that the first station is the most volatile. In 1983, the Coalinga earthquake in California occurred on the exact day of Mercury's first station in May, the downing of the Korean airliner by the Soviets on the exact day of Mercury's first station in September, and the collision of two jets on a runway in Alaska on the exact day of Mercury's first station in December. In October 1987, the stock market dropped 500 points beginning on the day that Mercury stationed.

See Appendix C for a table of the dates when Mercury stations, retrogrades, moves direct, and finally passes its first station. Listed also are the degrees of the signs where Mercury will be located.

Chapter 11:

Predicting with Transits

The natal (birthchart) positions of planets will always be sensitive points for an individual. As life goes on and the planets move ahead in their orbits, they occupy (or make aspects to) these sensitive points in the birthchart. "Transits" are the connections that form between the present-day planetary positions and those that occurred at the time and place of birth. The "transiting" planet essentially re-activates a "natal" planet.

For example, suppose that the Sun's position at birth was 12 degrees of Scorpio. In June, 1984, Mars passed through 12 degrees of Scorpio. This connection between the Sun at birth and Mars in 1984 constitutes what is called a transit, expressed in astrology as "transiting Mars conjunct the natal Sun." Because Mars is associated with activity, assertiveness, and friction, one could say that in June, 1984, anyone born with the Sun near 12 degrees of Scorpio was likely to find their lives more active than normal and possibly quite stressful.

The transiting planet brings its qualities to the natal planet that it contacts in the birthchart. Often, just being in the same or opposite sign as the Sun, Moon, or Ascendant is enough for the trend symbolized by the transiting planet to become readily apparent. This is particularly true of the transits made by the slower-moving planets.

The mechanism for this (exactly how the transits are able to affect us) is unclear at present. It appears that transits release the contents of the natal chart in certain ways. They seem to trigger the "printed circuits" of our birthcharts in some strange way that steers our experiences in a direction specified by the symbolism involved. The time lag between the transit and the experience can vary. Some people seem to respond immediately to a transit, others respond after a delay. It is possible that transits activate brain circuits that move us to register more vividly the things that are symbolized by the transiting and transited planets. In other words, transits create highlights in our consciousness that cause us to move towards or away from specific stimuli. Since an explanation for how astrology really works is years away, this is just an hypothesis.

Learning About Transits: An Exercise

Because we can calculate the positions of all the transiting planets well into the future, we can predict trends in a person's life experience. Such information can help give structure to the otherwise seemingly arbitrary changes in a person's life. Below is a set of guidelines for working with a birthchart and the exact positions of the transiting planets. It is quite easy to learn this approach to understanding the future (as well as the past and present). Readers who have a facility for geometry will be able to do the exercise completely in their heads.

If you decide to become your own astrologer, keep two things in mind. First, a forecasting system based only on transits is limited and may not account for all the changes and developments that a person may experience. There are other, more complex systems that must be combined with transits in order to get the full picture. Second, it can take up to a year to begin to grasp the way life works when viewed from the astrological perspective. You may need to revise some of your assumptions about how things work. If you follow the rules, do the homework, and give some real thought to what you observe, you will acquire a useful tool that will serve you well when you use it with understanding and restraint. The basic rules are as follows:

1. Have an accurate birthchart calculated, either by a competent astrologer or from an astrological computing service.

2. Buy an ephemeris (book of planetary tables). This will allow you to determine the position (zodiacal longitude) of any planet on any day. Recommended: *The American Ephemeris* (midnight version), by Astro Communications Services.

3. Buy a book that delineates the various transits. Recommended: *Planets in Transit* by Robert Hand.

4. Construct a sensitive point catalog for your own birthchart. This is a list of the degree and minute of every aspect to every point in the birthchart, organized in zodiacal order. With this list, you can easily determine transits to planetary positions in the natal chart. You may want to begin with only the five basic Ptolemaic aspects (the conjunction, sextile, square, trine, and opposition) and then later add others.

Here is an example of how to start a sensitive point catalog. Suppose that the natal Moon is located at 15 degrees and 30 minutes Aries. This sensitive point will be transited by the following aspects:

conjunction at 15 degrees 30 minutes of Aries (15♈30);
opposition (180 degrees away) in Libra at 15♎30;
square (90 degrees away) in Cancer - Capricorn at 15♋30 or 15♑30.
trine (120 degrees away) at 15♌30 or 15♐30,
and the sextile (60 degrees away) at 15♊30 or 15♒30.

After you calculate all the aspect positions for all the natal planets, plus the Ascendant and Midheaven, arrange them in the order of the zodiac signs, starting with Aries. Then, if you were to look in the ephemeris one day and find that Mars is passing through the sign of Leo, you could turn to your section of Leo listings and determine what connections transiting Mars would be making to your birthchart. You could also determine the days on which these transits would happen.

5. Do some basic personal research. First, make a list of major events in your life and then correlate them with the positions of the transiting planets at those times. Second, determine when transiting planets were aspecting your birthchart, and then correlate this information with what was actually happening in your life at that time. Use an orb of one degree for the slower-moving outer planets. Only by working carefully with your own chart will you begin to understand clearly the kind of response you have to each planet. Don't be surprised if you seem to experience the effects of a transit a few days before or after it is exact. Every person will respond somewhat differently to a given transit. A professional astrologer uses his or her experience and takes this into account. You can become very competent at interpreting your own birthchart if you follow these suggestions.

6. In a calendar or datebook, write down the transits to your chart on the appropriate days. While the faster-moving planets may register trends and events on the day they make an exact aspect, give the slower-moving planets a week or two to make their presence felt. Do this for a month or two in advance. As time passes, make notes of what happened. Read about the transits as you live through them. Do not attempt to predict for yourself or to alter your plans radically until you have mastered these basics of calculation and observation. Keep your eyes open and you will enter the world of astrological symbolism.

The Transits of the Planets

As the planets move through their orbits, they make aspects to the degree-positions that they were in at birth. Each transiting planet has a general effect described below. The specific effects of a given transit are shown by the natal planet it aspects, the nature of the aspect being made, the natal planet's house and sign position, and any other aspects that natal planet receives. Another variable to consider is that all transits will be technically exact at some point, but not all will produce effects right at that time. In general, the slower a planet moves, the more power it has on the birthchart. When planets are about to turn retrograde or direct, their motions are particularly slow and their effects become very strong. These nearly motionless points where the planets turn around are called *stations*. The effects of a transit of fast-moving Mercury will normally amount to very little, but when it stations it has the power of Jupiter or Saturn.

Sun: The Sun livens up whatever planet it is transiting, and it will emphasize the function of the transited planet for a day or two near the time the transit is exact. Often, authority and leadership issues are raised by the Sun's transit.

Moon: Lunar transits are quick, often lasting only a few hours. In some cases, clearly discernible events occur within just a few minutes of the Moon's exact aspect to a natal planet. Most Moon transits are subtle, but they do effect people on subconscious levels and will generally stimulate feelings, needs, or desires that lead them to change what they are doing at the time.

New and Full Moons: At the new Moon the Sun and the Moon occupy the same degree for about an hour. If this degree is the same as that of a natal planet, Ascendant, or Midheaven, the new Moon is then a double transit and its effects can be quite noticeable. A new Moon exactly conjunct a point in the birthchart will activate that point strongly, forcing attention to the issues symbolized for several days. The same is true for the full Moon, though in this case two opposite points become simultaneous transits. *Eclipses* are precisely focused new and full Moons which pack even more power. Their effects can last for months.

Mercury: Mercury brings out the need to use our minds, to communicate and to negotiate the world around us. Mercury transits are quick, lasting only a day or two. When Mercury stations during its retrograde movement, however, its effects become far more powerful. Mercury transits emphasize communications and transportation. Calls, talks, messages, paperwork, writing, and information processing become emphasized and tend to require more attention. Also, transportation matters including driving, riding, walking, and mobility in general, become prominent themes or pressing issues.

Venus: Venus brings out the need to meet, join, harmonize with, and generally relate to others. Social interactions are increased or emphasized when this planet is transiting over important parts of a birthchart. Venus transits coincide with meetings, gatherings, parties, consultations, and any partner-related events. People also feel a need to get involved with others when under a Venus transit and will make efforts to do so in one form or another. Persons with artistic, decorative or fashion interests will be active in these areas during a Venus transit. Although a typical Venus transit may last only a day or two, Venus in retrograde motion will emphasize the part of the birthchart it passes through for several months.

Mars: The need to move personal agendas forward and get thing done is stimulated under Mars transits. Common themes during a Mars transit are energetic activity, quick reactions, and conflicts. People experiencing a Mars transit will become busier, more energetic, more self-directed, more determined, and more assertive. They will be moved to take the initiative and not wait for others to do things first. Mars transits will coincide with construction projects, competitions, sports and athletic events. Mars transits can be challenging and some people will struggle with self-control issues. Impulsive actions and obliviousness to the existence of other people sometimes results in arguments, conflicts, and even accidents. Mars transits generally last for at least several days.

Jupiter: This planet brings increases and growth. Positively, a Jupiter transit stimulates confidence and optimism, bringing opportunities and abundance. Jupiter transits stimulate positive thinking on the "big-picture" level and can move people to do things based on what they believe to be right. Negatively, Jupiter transits coincide with excesses, too much of a good thing, and a tendency to blur the distinction between opinions and truth. Travel, learning, educational matters, philosophy, religion, and law may be a part of a Jupiter transit. Jupiter transits have an influence that generally lasts for a week or two, but in some cases for several months.

Saturn: Saturn transits bring pressures, responsibilities, and awareness of limits. During Saturn transits, people generally find that they have less freedom and more responsibility. Authority figures or high standards will normally figure into the transit's influence in some way. Saturn transits don't allow for sloppiness or avoidance, they demand quality, practicality, and solidity. People who have a hard time accepting delays, obstacles, and reality may become frustrated and depressed under a long Saturn transit. Others, more in touch with consensus reality, will "chop wood and carry water" during the duration of the transit and emerge from it with something substantial accomplished. Nothing moves fast during Saturn transits; these are times when patience and endurance become valuable assets. Saturn transits last for several months to a year.

Uranus: Disruptions and instability are the recognizable features of a Uranus transit. Uranus brings the need to change things and it is the process of change itself that creates disturbances and instability. Typical Uranus transits bring completely new experiences, temporary and unique conditions that can't be repeated, unusual events, reforms, revolutions, and rebellions. People often respond to Uranus by first being rigid, then suddenly making a change that surprises their friends and family. A Uranus transit will bring out a person's need for freedom of self-expression. If this is not acceptable to the people around them, they will either rebel or make an attempt to change things. Uranus transits work suddenly and sometimes quite unexpectedly. The actual events of a transit may last for about a week, the repercussions may last for several months or longer.

Neptune: Positively, Neptune transits make people more sensitive to the arts and music, more compassionate and spiritual. Negatively, they will make people feel confused and overwhelmed by life, and the response may be escapist behaviors, denial, or isolation. Complex and unclear circumstances are usually part of a Neptune transit. The challenge here is to move intuitively with the changes, to feel one's way through the complexities. Making sacrifices is part of the Neptunian theme. Neptune transits are good for volunteer work, spiritual matters, the arts, and the exploration of states of consciousness. The effects of major Neptune transits can be felt for months and even years.

Pluto: Pluto transits are very powerful and typically coincide with lifestyle changes and psychological crises. Pluto moves people to let go of situations in their life that are blocking personal evolution. On a deeper level Pluto challenges people to change their thinking and their internal programing (the psychological mechanism that attracts them to troublesome situations or people in the first place). Pluto transits mark periods of time when people are forced into accepting transformations. They coincide with births, marriages, deaths, divorces, financial crises both positive and negative, psychological growth or challenges, investigations, eliminations, and renewals. Since Pluto moves so slowly, its transits last for a year, sometimes several years.

The Seven-Year Cycle

The so-called seven-year itch is a popular expression for a cycle that is shown astrologically by the transits of the planet Saturn. Saturn takes (on the average) 29.4 years to pass through all 12 signs of the zodiac. Dividing this period into quarters yields segments of 7.3 years each, when Saturn reaches the quarter, half, three-quarter, and completion points of its cycle.

Beginning at birth, there are successive periods of about seven years in a person's life, each one a stage of important adjustments to reality. At about 7 years of age, the first quarter of the transiting Saturn cycle, the first crisis of maturity occurs and self-awareness takes form. At about ages 14 or 15, the change from child to adult occurs. About 22 years of age brings another adjustment to the demands of society. When Saturn completes its first cycle at about 29 years, people must come to terms with themselves and the society in which they live. This point in the cycle is called the *Saturn return*. It is almost always a time of important commitments, decisions, and the acceptance of responsibilities.

The next stages of the Saturn cycle occur at around the ages of 37, 44 (the peak of the mid-life crisis), and 52. Saturn again returns to its original position at about age 59. This second Saturn return is usually experienced more positively than the first, since most people are more settled and realistic at this point in life. The Saturn cycle marks the rhythms of maturity, reality, security, and responsibility in any number of human activities. Crisis points can be observed in relationships or marriages at 7.3 years after the first meeting or the wedding. A store owner may need to make crucial business decisions 14.6 years after opening, and so forth.

The Graphic Ephemeris

The transits of the planets throughout the year can be shown visually on what is called a graphic ephemeris. On the graph below (a six-month 30-degree graphic ephemeris print-out from Astrolabe's *Timegraphs* software) the vertical scale indicates the degrees from 0 to 30. The horizontal scale shows the months of the year. If a planet is at 10 degrees of a sign in July, and travels to 20 degrees of that sign by December, its passage is shown as a diagonal line across the graph. The outer planets, which move very slowly, are easy to spot on the graph because their lines change gradually. The inner planets are shown by lines that are often just short of being vertical. Mercury, for example, can travel the full 30 degrees of a sign in less than a month.

You can track the transits against your own chart by drawing horizontal lines across the graph at the degrees of the planets and points in your natal chart. For example, if you have the Sun at 15 degrees of Aries, you would draw a line through the 15 degree mark. By locating where the lines of the transiting planets cross the lines of your natal chart, you can determine when a transit will occur. Because the graph is only 30 degrees (the 12 signs are collapsed into one), you will have to determine just what aspect is being made. The following aspects are possible using this graph: conjunction, semisextile, sextile, square, trine, quincunx and opposition. A crossing of a planet line could be a conjunction, or a sextile or opposition; only the name of the signs involved will tell you which one.

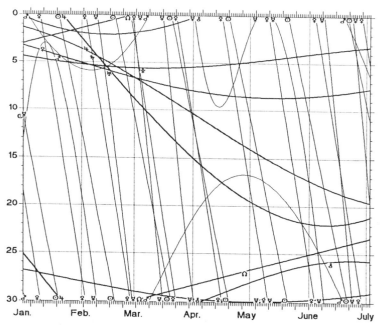

There is another popular graphic ephemeris (not shown here) that is based on a 45-degree modulus. In this graph, the vertical column goes from 0 degrees to 45 degrees. In terms of the zodiac it goes from 0 degrees of the Cardinal signs to 15 degrees of the Fixed signs, and/or from 15 degrees of the Fixed signs to 0 degrees of the Cardinal signs. Using this graph, you can locate transits to the natal chart in any one of the following aspects: conjunction, semisquare, square, sesquiquadrate and opposition. Again, you will have to look at the signs involved in order to determine exactly which aspect is being formed.

Symbolic Substitution

Anyone who follows the transits to their natal chart for a few months will come to the conclusion that they work. It will also become obvious that no two transits involving the same planets will result in the same effect, yet whatever transpires is always within the limits of the symbolism involved. Mars transiting the natal Moon, for example, may at one time coincide with a conflict with a woman. At another time there might be a home repair with associated hammer-banging. At another time, there may be a stomach upset caused by too many red hot peppers. The Mars/Moon symbolism is consistent in all three events -- Mars is anger, force, and irritation, while the Moon is female, home, and stomach. But how do we know which form a transit will take?

Most probably, transits activate forces deep within us that manifest in whatever symbolically-appropriate forms are immediately available. In the case of Mars transiting the Moon, some sense of urgency (Mars) is felt in the subconscious security system (Moon). When these forces rise to the surface of consciousness, they manifest with the appropriate symbols. Isn't it possible, then, to use free-will to choose what form the symbols might take? The astrological theory of Symbolic Substitution suggests exactly that. Because we can anticipate exactly when a transit will occur, we can steer ourselves toward more productive manifestations of the planetary energies.

Since we know that Mars will be transiting the Moon, it is possible to deliberately create a Mars-Moon event. For instance, plan to do something active or constructive with a woman, or perhaps paint the house red, or maybe set up a situation where one can vent anger in an appropriate manner. This is electional astrology at its finest -- being creative with free-will, but staying with-in the context of the symbolism.

Other Astrological Predictive Techniques

Transits are only one of a number of methodologies that astrologers use to evaluate trends and make forecasts. One of the oldest predictive techniques is called *Directions*, in which angles of the birthchart are "directed" to the planets in the birthchart at a specific rate. In essence, this technique takes the birthchart and moves it ahead, correlating one degree of motion at the Midheaven to one year of life. It is the rotation of the Earth after the birth moment that is measured when using directions. If a chart has the Midheaven at 10 degrees of Libra, and Saturn is located at 15 degrees of Libra, then the Midheaven would be directed to Saturn at age 5 - and a corresponding trend would occur.

Another technique is *Secondary Progressions*. This popular predictive system uses the correlation of a day-for-a-year to determine how a person might experience any given year. If the person is 45 years old, the planetary positions on the 45th day after birth are examined. By working with proportions, very exact forecasts can be made.

Using *Solar Arcs* is a technique which involves finding the distance between the progressed Sun and the natal Sun at the rate of one day-for-a-year, and then applying it to the other planets. This technique, popularized by the Hamburg School of Astrology (Uranian Astrology) is a form of secondary progressions.

Another technique, *Solar Returns*, is the construction of charts cast for the exact moment in any year that the Sun returns to its exact birth position. These charts offer information about the year ahead. The same technique is used with the Moon to calculate *Lunar Returns*, charts that are read for the month ahead. Astrologers vary in their methodologies. Some favor solar and lunar returns, other don't use them at all. There is no single way to do astrological forecasting.

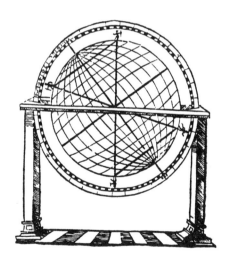

Chapter 12:

Doing Astrology On a Computer

Since the early 1980s it has been possible to work with astrology on a personal computer. For the first time in history, the laborious work of the calculations necessary to make horoscopes, transits, and progressions is no longer a major block to learning astrology. In many respects, the computer has made astrology more democratic and beyond the domain of the purely mathematically minded.

Astrology software was among the earliest commercial software made, and it has revolutionized this subject in ways that were previously unimaginable. It seems that the computer has done for astrology what electricity did for the guitar -- given it more power and brought it to a much wider audience. Since the introduction of microcomputers in the 1970s, the evolution of computer hardware, software, and peripherals has been remarkably rapid and shows no signs of slowing down. Because of this, the material in this chapter will become dated very quickly, unlike the rest of this book.

This marriage between astrology and the personal computer has created a number of interesting possibilities. People who have access to a computer can explore many facets of astrology with great ease. Much like a carpenter's toolbox, a good astrological program can provide many tools that are specific to the task needed to be done. Before computers, many of these astrological tools were inaccessible.

Some astrology computer programs are aimed at the professional practitioner who may use high-powered techniques and methods. Other types of software can be used by less sophisticated astrologers (or non-astrologers) to earn money by producing printed astrological reports. Some software allows users with astrological knowledge to take raw data from astrology programs and add interpretations of their own. This lets the user sell their own personally customized reports. Some software is aimed solely at the non-astrologer. This type of software lets the user create personal astrological reports that are built from previously prepared text blocks written by an astrologer.

At the time of this writing (1997), most of the software written for astrology is designed to be run on IBM-compatible (DOS and Windows) or Apple Macintosh computers. If you have a computer that is not one of these, don't be discouraged. There is probably some astrology software out there for your machine. Astrological software was among the first software available for personal computers. If you have an old or odd machine, call the software companies listed in Appendix D. Chances are good that someone has already written something for it. If you are thinking of purchasing a computer for use with astrological software (or any software, for that matter), keep the following information in mind:

IBMs or IBM-compatibles have been the computers most widely supported by astrological software companies, with more software of all varieties available for this type of computer than for any other. There is also a lot of competition among software companies that write for this kind of computer and they compete mainly on features and price.

With IBMs or clones, most astrological software can run on simple systems, such as an XT with a hard disk. With an Apple Macintosh, the latest and most advanced machines of this type are generally required to run the current versions of astrological software written for those machines. The Apple Macintosh is simply more expensive for the amount of computing power needed for astrology software. Even if you purchase an older or used IBM compatible, you can expect reasonable performance and inexpensive service and repair charges. It is not wise to purchase an old Apple Macintosh because you will probably not get acceptable performance or inexpensive repair service.

If you plan on purchasing a used computer, consider the following. Get one equipped with a 386DX chip or better, a hard disk with at least 130 megabytes of storage, 4 megabytes of RAM (internal computer memory), a fast graphics card, and a non-interlaced, shielded color monitor. This is not as expensive as it sounds because computers are now a commodity item and are very inexpensive. Used or outdated computers can often be purchased for unbelievably low prices.

For many years, most IBM-compatibles operated in an environment called MS-DOS. This has changed. Today the Microsoft Windows program runs on top of MS-DOS and allows access to an array of astounding programs. Windows has opened up an entirely new vista in personal computing, with the appearance of more and more astrological and non-astrological Windows programs.

Today's astrological software can be divided into several basic categories. Your choice of software depends on your intentions, though you may have several interests that can be accommodated by one large program. There are a number of companies that produce astrological software and you can order from them directly (see Appendix D). There are also distributors that carry many packages from various companies. Apart from the individual differences between the various software publishers, most astrological software on the market today falls within one of the following categories.

Low-End Introductory Software

These programs are excellent for beginners and for those who simply want to calculate a chart or read interpretive text from the screen. Typically, these programs do not print any charts or text, though you can usually print what is on the screen by using certain keys on your keyboard. They are designed for browsing through a chart, looking at aspects or perhaps reading paragraphs that describe some of the chart's main features. One thing that should be stressed about these programs is that their calculations are usually very precise and you can count on the charts they produce to be accurate. The better programs in this category range from $25 to $75. Examples are *Astro-Deluxe* published by Halloran Software, and *Kaleidoscope* and *E-Z Charts* from Matrix.

There are also a few shareware programs available from electronic bulletin boards that may serve your purpose. Most of these are quite inexpensive, but accuracy is questionable and they may not run as smoothly or be designed as professionally as the packages produced by the larger astrological software developers.

High-End Delineation Packages -- Report Writers

These programs are highly specialized and offer quality astrological delineations that can be printed and bound into reports. Most individuals who purchase this type of software do so because they want to sell astrological reports, and some have earned considerable amounts doing so. In some cases the software producers offer valuable suggestions, even graphics, to help end-users get started in business. Report-writing programs are available for all major types of astrological delineation. Most popular are those that print delineations of the natal chart. Many of these print out the horoscope itself first and then sort out the relative weights of factors such as the elements, qualities and planetary distributions (much like what is described in Chapter 9). Then the programs delineate the chart planet-by-planet, house by house. By attaching a nicely designed front and back cover, and using a simple binding, the user of such a program can produce an attractive and helpful product, or gift, to interested friends and family.

Other report writers are available for relationships, including both synastry and the composite chart, progressions, transits, solar and lunar returns, and even this author's Maya/Aztec Astrology program. For many, the reports generated by these programs are an excellent way to learn astrology and to follow the constantly changing trends in one's life. Prices are typically between $200 to $400, depending on the complexity of the program and the amount of text that is produced. Some programs are designed to be compatible with other programs, usually those produced by the same manufacturer, and can read the chart files of those programs, thus speeding up data entry.

The text to the many delineation packages on the market is built into the program and is usually written by a known astrologer or one with a flair for concise expression. In some cases, you may have a choice of authors or a choice of different texts, each slanted differently. Another option is to write the text yourself. Using an editor program supplied by the software company, you can get into the text database and re-compose delineations to suit your own style of thinking. With a little effort you can personalize and customize an astrological report in a way that sets it apart from all others.

Examples of report-writing software are *Professional Natal Report* and *Professional Forecaster* from Astrolabe, or *Friends and Lovers* from Matrix. Cosmic Pattern's *Kepler* program prints reports and also does calculations like the programs described in the next section.

High-End Calculation Packages

These programs are for professionals who want the top-of-the-line software. Although they don't all print reports, they offer every conceivable kind of calculation known to astrologers. The chart printouts are usually of excellent quality and it is these programs that are used by those who run chart calculation services -- making charts for other astrologers. One of the real services to astrologers that these programs offer is the freedom to test out techniques. Over the centuries, numerous predictive and analytical techniques have been created and utilized by astrologers, and in many cases no general consensus has ever been reached as to their validity or usefulness. With these programs, users can test for themselves if asteroids, Ascendant arcs, or fixed stars work for them. In this sense, the computer has really opened all facets of astrology to testing by eliminating the incredibly time-consuming calculations necessary for most techniques.

Programs in this category usually cost about as much as the text writing programs in the $150-to-$400 range. But you get a lot for your money. Examples in this category are programs like Astrolabe's top-rated *Solar Fire* and *Nova, Winstar* and *Blue Star* from Matrix, *Pathfinder* from ACI, *Star Trax* from AIR Software, and *Astro-Deluxe for Windows* from Halloran Software.

Research Programs

One of the major problems that the field of astrology has faced over the past 300 years has been the lack of hard proof that it actually works. As described in Chapter 4, a major stumbling block for astrology was that proof by statistical analysis wasn't possible during the Scientific Revolution because those analytical techniques hadn't been invented yet. During this century a few statistical studies of astrology were done, but at great expense in time and money to individuals. Because establishment scientists and academics continue to ignore astrology (astrology is not politically correct at the present time), no money for research on the subject has been forthcoming. This is where a certain type of high-end calculation software comes in. For the first time in history, these programs allow individuals to do astrological research at a relatively low cost and with great potential benefit to the astrological and scientific communities. *ARP* from AIR Software and *JigSaw* from Astrolabe are examples of this type of software.

Professional Interactive Programs

Although these programs often offer many of the same options as the high-end calculation packages, they are designed primarily for users who require immediate responses to a wide number of options. For example, a program like Astrolabe Software's *Chartwheels* or Matrix's *Quick Charts* lets the user quickly put a chart up on the screen, then manipulate it instantaneously to fit the needs of the moment. Such options are extremely valuable when doing horary astrology (answering questions as they are posed) or electional astrology (finding the best time to begin an action of one sort or another). When a birth time is unknown, a birth time search is made much easier with this type of software. More than anything else, interactive programs let the user experiment with astrology. Prices are usually somewhat lower than high-end calculation packages. It is in this category that astrology software users can come closest to doing hands-on astrology. The immediate response to data entry allows for a kind of dialogue between user and machine.

Being able to access a quick answer to a question by reference to a chart for the moment (horary astrology), or to simply glance at where the planets are now, brings astrology closer to life. Having a chart for the present moment on screen (updating itself every ten seconds) can show amazing correlations with the world around us. Sometimes Mars will reach the Midheaven and at that moment the sound of a police siren or some loud noises will be heard; or when Uranus rises, a disruptive phone call comes through. Programs like *Nostradamus* and *Father Time* from AIR Software have been designed for quick work with horary and electional astrology.

Specialized Astrology Programs

The field of astrology is really quite vast, as big as any other subject taught in the colleges and universities, and there are a number of topics that require special software. One of the more popular branches of natal astrology today is astro-mapping. By casting a birthchart for a locality other than that of birth, a different set of houses is derived, and therefore a different planetary emphasis is created (see Chapter 8). Further, this information can be displayed graphically on a map, or on screen, and one can judge how visiting or moving to a particular location might be experienced. Today there are software packages that are strictly limited to the computations needed for the various methods of astro-mapping, though these usually require graphics capability in your computer. Astrolabe's *Solar Maps* and Matrix's *AstroMap Hi-Res* are examples of such software packages.

For hundreds of years astrologers have examined the positions of the planets placed on a circle called the horoscope. Due to the graphics capability of modern computers, some programs offer alternatives to this perspective. Arranging planetary data in graph form lets one see more than just one moment in time -- a graph makes the birthchart visibly dynamic. Such a revolution in astrology was really not possible without much effort and hand calculations until the advent of the personal computer. Astrologers now have power tools that their predecessors never dreamed of. Astrolabe's *Timegraphs* is an example in this category of software.

Other specialty areas include programs that let users explore astrological traditions other than those of the Western world. Software from several producers is now available for Hindu (Vedic) astrology, a complex tradition that has never lost favor in India. The astrology of the Maya and Aztecs is the subject of *Maya/Aztec Astro-Report*, an

Astrolabe program which is both screen-interactive and report-generating. As the author of the interpretation portion of this program, I can testify to its versatility and uniqueness among software packages.

Miscellaneous Software

Also available is a type of software called a TSR which resides in your computer's memory and can be called upon whenever you need it, regardless of what program you are running. Astrolabe's *Solar Sparks* is such a program. By simply pressing two keys, you can get a chart of the moment on a portion of your screen. With another keystroke, you get the aspects of the current planets. In some respects, this is like having access to a constantly moving astrological clock.

Another useful type of memory-resident software is one that contains birth data entry information, like the latitude, longitude and time zone for a birthplace. Since time-keeping has not been consistent throughout the world (because of man-made political and seasonal time shifting like Daylight Saving Time), it is far more convenient to access that information via a memory-resident program than through a long book search. Programs that contain such databases are large and will consume huge amounts of disk space, therefore requiring a hard disk. One such program is the *ACS PC Atlas* produced by Astro Communications Services.

Astrologers may also want to investigate software that has been written for amateur astronomers. A number of low-cost programs are available today that calculate eclipses and lunations, and some even draw star maps. Much of this information is also available using some of the high-end astrological calculation packages, but some users may find these smaller astronomical programs interesting. Since they are designed for those interested in astronomy, their astrological uses may be limited, but the difference in approach may also be a stimulus to creative thinking about our cosmic environment. Astrologers and those interested in astrology shouldn't make the same mistake that those in astronomy have by avoiding astrology. An open mind is a good thing. Zephyr Software sells several low-cost astronomy programs. You can also experiment with inexpensive shareware such as *SkyMap* and *SkyGlobe*, available from Andromeda Software, a reliable vendor of astronomy shareware.

Another type of program is one that creates high-quality output (i.e., beautiful charts) using existing chart files, but which performs few or no calculations. Programs, such as Astrolabe's *Printwheels*, can create over one hundred different chart forms, tables and dial-type charts using a dot, laser, inkjet, or PostScript device. Charts can be drawn in low, medium, or high resolution. The DTP versions of this type of software can be extremely powerful. These versions allow various chart forms and tables to be exported to graphic files which can be read by any popular word-processor or drawing program. This allows detailed astrological illustrations to be customized and incorporated into art works, books, magazines, or even tee-shirts.

Where to Buy Astrological Software

Purchasing astrological software is best done by telephone and mail-order because few computer software chainstores carry quality astrology programs. To begin, readers should write or call the software producers listed in Appendix D and ask for a catalog. Software may also be purchased through a distributor such as Microcycles. This company stocks software from the producers and sells it for the same prices you'd pay if you ordered directly from the company. Once you've decided on what type of program you're interested in purchasing, ask for a demo disk. Most companies offer demo disks that allow you to get a feel for their programs. Demo disks cost about $3 and will allow you to do some shopping at a very low cost.

Most of the software mentioned above is for IBM-type computers using DOS or Windows. Some of the software producers listed in Appendix D also sell some excellent programs made for the Apple Mac. Time Cycles Research is one company that specializes entirely in programs for the Mac and offers a collection programs, the Io Series, that fit most of the categories listed above. Astrolabe and Matrix also sell quality software for Apple Mac.

The future of astrology and computers is promising. As this technology becomes more powerful and easier to use, ideas that were once just dreams can become real and useful. In the future we may use expert systems whereby chart delineations read like that of an experienced astrologer. These programs will allow astrologers to transfer the exact way he or she reads a chart to the computer. The marriage of astrology and computers promises to be not only fruitful but a powerful one as well.

Appendix A:

The Astrological Reading

Having your birthchart read by a competent astrologer can be a powerful experience. It can help to give your life more structure by putting things into perspective, and it can suggest possible strategies for handling challenges. It may actually change your life. Astrology is a wonderful tool in the quest for self-knowledge, the foundation of all psychological and spiritual work. An astrological reading is like referring to a road map -- and maps are a great help when you need to be better organized or make choices about which route to take. They are especially valuable on those rare occasions when you are actually lost! But keep in mind that maps are kept most of the time in the glove compartment, not thrown across the windshield where they obscure your vision. Likewise, too much astrology can be worse than too little.

Before seeking out an astrologer and making an appointment, be sure that you know the date, place, and exact time of your birth. A birth time error of only four minutes can make a substantial difference, especially in forecasting. If your parents don't remember your time of birth, check with your state's bureau of vital statistics (usually in the state capital) and request a hospital birth record search. You will be asked to provide them with your name, birthdate, birthplace and parents' names. The fee for such a search is usually between $5 to $10 and takes about two weeks.

If your time of birth is completely unknown, you have two options. You could settle for what is called a solar chart reading. Here, the astrologer calculates a chart for sunrise on the day you were born and attempts to read it as if it were your birthchart. In many cases, the results of this approach are reasonably accurate and helpful. Your other option is to have an astrologer determine your time of birth through a process called *rectification*. Using a list of dates of major events in your life, the astrologer will attempt to adjust the chart to fit the events. Rectification is extremely complex, time-consuming and costly. Expect to pay far more for this service than for a reading.

Now, in possession of accurate birth data, you must find an astrologer to do a personal reading for you. Names of astrologers, and also other counselors and healers, are often found in community or regional directories dedicated to such practices. Astrological organizations will give references if you ask them. Some astrologers are listed in the phone book and some names may come to you by word of mouth. You may have heard of a local astrologer that has a good reputation or perhaps know of one that lives in another state but does telephone readings. Do you feel more comfortable meeting with an astrologer in person or would you prefer a phone consultation?

One way of deciding on an astrologer is to call and talk to him or her. You can often learn much in just a few moments of interaction. Be sure to assess his or her qualifications. How long has this astrologer been practicing? Is the astrologer a member of any astrological organizations? Has the astrologer bothered to take certification tests? Does he or she have a college degree? Any graduate degrees? Has he or she published anything? Do they teach classes? Does the astrologer have references? What is his or her philosophy of astrology? Keep in mind that many astrologers today are hobbyists, i.e., they practice astrology on the side. A few of these part-time practitioners are highly qualified and you may find their fees on the low side. As was mentioned in Chapter 2, certification tests are available to astrologers but, as with doctors, this is not a 100% guarantee of competency. Don't forget to ask about their fees, the length of their readings, and when they take appointments.

Having selected an astrologer and made an appointment, you may want to prepare yourself by reviewing some of the basic astrological concepts in this book. Making a list of the questions you have about yourself and your life would also be helpful. Be sure that your reading is recorded, either by the astrologer or yourself, so that you may review it later. Often, so much is said during a reading that it takes several playbacks to assimilate the material.

Your astrologer will prepare for the reading by calculating your birth-chart. Today, most astrologers use computers or computing services for this time-consuming job. Most astrologers will begin their reading of your chart with a discussion of your personality and life potentials. Using the positions of the planets in signs and houses, the astrologer will ascertain your life pattern from the symbols. Be patient, it may take a while for the astrologer to put it all together, but that's because each person is uniquely complex. (Compare this to the number of sessions it takes the typical psychotherapist to understand a person this thoroughly.) There is no single, universally approved format for reading charts. Some astrologers may wish to spend an entire session on just the birthchart alone and request that you schedule another session for predictive work. Others may combine both subjects in one reading. You will need to ask the astrologer ahead of time how he or she prefers to work.

While having your chart read, feel free to ask questions and provide what may be relevant information. Without your input and feedback, the astrologer may not be able to locate which of several possibilities within a general category is the right one for you. This is the same technique as a doctor uses; knowing that you hurt, the doctor asks you exactly where it hurts and what kind of pain it is. Interactive dialogue between astrologer and client can be very productive, but let the astrologer do most of the talking.

Ask your astrologer about any other services he or she offers. Besides personality readings and forecasting, many astrologers today will analyze all types of relationships, including marriage, business partnerships, and parent/child relations. By comparing two birthcharts, and also deriving a composite or relationship chart for the two, much can be learned about the potential of a relationship even before it has begun!

Your location on this earth can make a difference in your life. Some astrologers will be able to assess your potential in other places, using the techniques of locational astrology. Ask if your astrologer is certified in this field or has worked with it extensively. Horary astrology, the art of reading a chart cast for the time a critical question was asked, and electional astrology, the choice of a best time to do something, are specialty areas that your astrologer (or another) may be experienced in. Also, many astrologers publish newsletters and sell low-cost computer generated readings.

Each astrologer has his or her own orientation and way of working. Although most astrologers in this country practice Western astrology, some incorporate elements of other traditions, such as Vedic or Hindu astrology. Astrologers may specialize or combine it with Western astrology. (I utilize some components of Mesoamerican astrology in my primarily Western astrological practice.) When it comes to forecasting, a number of techniques are available to astrologers. Most often used are transit positions of the current planets (compared to the birthchart) and progressions (a symbolic day-for-a-year method of timing life's events). Other forecasting techniques are solar and lunar returns, solar arc directions, and primary directions. In the hands of an expert, any of these techniques will work well.

Astrologers, like all counselors or consultants, differ philosophically. Some are psychologically oriented while others emphasize the spiritual side of life's events. Some are idealistic while others are pragmatic. Some are more fatalistic while others are more concerned with correct timing and making life run more efficiently. In the final analysis, there are as many kinds of astrologers as there are doctors or therapists. You'll have to determine which one is best for you.

Appendix B:

Calculating a Horoscope

Back in the 1960s, I used to do chart calculations with tables of proportions that I made myself. Later, I used either tables of logarithms or a slide rule. Then, in 1980, there was a "Master Class" held on Cape Cod and sponsored by the Cape Cod NCGR chapter. At least a hundred people turned out for this week-long seminar on astrological math and astronomy. Rob Hand was a principal lecturer, along with Steve Blake, Gary Christen, and others. For what most would regard as a boring topic for a seminar, the event turned out to be a grand success. There was even a test on the last day to see how much we learned. One of the things I learned from this event was how to do chart calculations on a scientific calculator. In my opinion, this is the best way to draw up a chart by hand today and I'm laying out the routines below in hopes that it will help some people get through the math part of an astrological certification test.

What you need: A midnight ephemeris, an astrological atlas (with latitudes, longitudes and Daylight Savings Time information), a scientific calculator, a pencil and a piece of paper. A table of houses is optional but useful. The scientific calculator is the key tool. It should have the trigonometric functions and an easy way of changing degrees and minutes into decimals, as well as the reverse. It should have at least one memory. You should be able to get one of these for under $20. Practice changing degrees (and minutes and seconds) to decimals and back again. Get the store salesman to show you how to do this before you buy the calculator. All of the important calculations in this method are done with decimals, not degrees.

You will also need to understand that the answers you will get from the calculator for the Midheaven, Ascendant, and houses will be expressed in true longitude. This means degrees, minutes, and seconds ranging from 0 to 360 starting at 0 Aries. Below is a list of signs, and the degrees they begin with, which you should become familiar with. To convert a figure in true longitude to zodiacal sign and degree, simply subtract the closest lesser value below. Example: 118 degrees. 90 (Cancer) is the closest lesser value, so 118 minus 90 equals 28, or 28 degrees of Cancer.

Aries: 0	Leo: 120	Sagittarius: 240
Taurus: 30	Virgo: 150	Capricorn: 270
Gemini: 60	Libra: 180	Aquarius: 300
Cancer: 90	Scorpio: 210	Pisces: 330

What you will be doing:

A. Finding the GMT of birth.
B. Finding the LST of birth.
C. Calculating the Midheaven.
D. Calculating the Ascendant.
E. Calculating the houses.
F. Calculating the planets' positions.

A: Finding the Greenwich Mean Time (GMT) of birth
(also called the Universal Time (UT) of birth)

1. Note the time of birth and correct it for daylight time (if it was in effect). This is usually minus 1 hour. Express the birth time in terms of 24 hours (military time).

2. *Add* the time zone difference for west longitude. Eastern Standard Time = +5 hours, CST = +6, etc. *Subtract* time zone difference for east longitudes.

3. This figure is the GMT. If it is greater than 24, subtract 24 and use the next day as the date of birth. Express it decimal form:

Example: January 1, 1994 at 12:01 AM (midnight or 0 hours) in NYC
(time zone 5):   TIME (00:01) + Zone (5) = 5:01
                   (expressed in decimals, = 5.0166). This is the GMT.

B. Finding the Local Sidereal Time (LST) of birth.

1. Find what's called the *Acceleration Correction* (AC) by taking the GMT (expressed in decimal form) and dividing it by 6.1. Then divide this figure by 60. (You could also figure it the old fashioned, slightly inaccurate, way by counting 10 seconds per hour of GMT. The answer in either case should always be under 4 minutes). Set this figure aside for now.

2. From the ephemeris, find the *Sidereal Time* (ST) at midnight on the day of birth. (Use the next day if the GMT was over 24 as in explained in step A3). Express it in decimal form.

3. Add the GMT, AC, and ST. (GMT + AC + ST).

4. Subtract the *Longitude Time Equivalent* (LTE) from the figure above. This LTE is found by dividing the longitude (expressed in decimals) by 15 or simply looking it up in a longitudes and latitudes book for astrologers. (In the Astro Communications Services Atlas, this is the last set of numbers listed -- but you'll still have to convert it to decimals). If the birth occurred in east longitude, you will *add* the LTE instead of subtracting it. If greater than 24, subtract 24.

5. You should now have the LST of the birth (in decimal form). The LST shows what sign is at the Midheaven. When the LST is 0.00, then 0 degrees of Aries is at the Midheaven. Normally, a table of houses is used to determine the Midheaven, Ascendant, and intermediate houses from the LST, but for the exact figures needed to pass a professional certification test this requires some cumbersome interpolation. The following method, using trigonometry, is really much easier. Just organize your numbers and push the right buttons.

Example: GMT (5.0166) + AC
               (GMT divided first by 6.1 and then by 60 = 0.0137)
    + ST   (6:41:40 converted to decimals is 6.6944)
    - LTE (4:55:48 converted to decimals is 4.93)
    = LST (6.7947)

Summary: Birth Time +/- Zone = GMT
                 GMT + AC + ST - LTE = LST

C. Calculating the Midheaven

1. Take the LST from step B5 and multiply by 15. This will give you the *Right Ascension of the Midheaven* (RAMC) which is the location of the Midheaven on the celestial equator. We will use trigonometry to relocate it to the ecliptic, or Sun's path, along which the zodiac extends. Put this figure, the RAMC, in the calculator's memory.

2. With the RAMC displayed, press TAN (tangent) on the calculator, then divide by the cosine of 23.45 (the Earth's tilt or *Obliquity* [OBL] of the ecliptic -- if you have a second memory, store this in it). The sequence on most calculators should be (starting with the RAMC in the display) TAN (divide) 23.45 COS (equals).

3. Now press either ARC TAN or TAN-1, whichever one your calculator has. Don't worry, they're the same thing with different names. On

many calculators, this will require first pressing an F or INV key (for second function or inverse function) and then ARC TAN or TAN-1. You now have a figure that may need to be adjusted. Check your original LST and if this LST is between 0 and 6, add nothing; between 6 and 18, add 180; and between 18 and 24, add 360.

4. Convert the result back into degrees and minutes and you should have the Midheaven. Check it against a table of houses or a computer printout.

Summary: The formula for calculating the Midheaven is:

$$MC = ARC\ TAN \frac{TAN\ RAMC}{COS\ OBL}$$

Example:
1. LST (6.7947) multiply (x) 15 equals (=) RAMC (101.9212).
2. Next, TAN divide (÷) 23.45 COS equals (=)
3. ARC TAN plus (+) 180 equals (=) Midheaven (100.9614 in decimals). Converting to degrees, minutes and seconds, the Midheaven is 100 degrees, 57 minutes and 41 seconds. Since the sign Cancer starts with 90 degrees (see table above) this corresponds to 10 Cancer 57 at the Midheaven. Compare this with a computer calculated chart.

D. Calculating the Ascendant

This is the toughest calculation because it requires so many buttons to be pushed impeccably. I won't even show you the formula until after it's over. But before you begin, make sure you have your RAMC in the memory of the calculator, and the obliquity (23.45) and the geographical latitude of the birth (also expressed in decimals) handy. If your calculator has extra memory, you should probably use it for these two latter constants. You should also make sure that you know where the parentheses are on your calculator. In the formula we are using, the proper use of the parentheses is critical.

1. Press the left-handed parenthesis key, input the latitude and press TAN. Press multiply (x), input the obliquity (OBL) and press SIN. Then press the right-handed parenthesis key.

2. Press the plus (+) sign. Next, press the left-handed parenthesis key again, recall the RAMC (or punch it in) and hit SIN. Press multiply (x), input the obliquity (OBL) again and press COS. Next, press the right-handed parenthesis key and press equals (=).

3. Now press the divide (÷) sign and recall (or punch in) the RAMC and press COS. Press the equals (=) sign.

4. Next, press the change signs (+/-) key and then the 1/X key (you may need to press a second function key to get to this one). Then press ARC TAN or TAN-1, whichever your calculator uses and take a good look at what you've got.

5. Now check your original LST. If it is greater than 0 and somewhere between 12.0 to 14.0, add 180. The exact change point will depend on your latitude. The change is around 13.25 for 40 degrees north. If the figure is over this value (12.0 to 14.0) and under 18.0, add 360. If it is over 18.00 and less than 24, add nothing.

6. After making the above correction, change your figure into degrees and minutes and locate the sign it falls in. You've got the Ascendant! Check it against a table of houses or computer printout.

Summary: The formula for calculating the Ascendant is:

$$1/X \text{ ARC TAN } - \frac{(TAN \text{ lat. } x \text{ SIN OBL}) + (SIN \text{ RAMC } x \text{ COS OBL})}{COS \text{ RAMC}}$$

Example:
The RAMC for the example above (January 1, 1994 at 12:01 AM in NYC) is 101.9212. The obliquity (OBL) is 23.45 and the geographical latitude is 40.7333 degrees north latitude.

1. Use your latitude and the OBL. Don't forget the parentheses! Input (40.7333 TAN X 23.45 SIN). You should have 0.34269 in your display.

2. Press plus (+) and then, using the parentheses again, input (101.9212 SIN X 23.45 COS). Hit the equals (=) key. You should have 1.2403 in the display.

3. Press divide, then recall or input the RAMC, hit COS and then equals (=). You should now have -6.0044 in the display.

4. Now hit the change signs key (+/-) and then the 1/X key. Next hit ARC TAN or TAN-1. Your display should read 9.4554.

5. Since this figure is above 0 but less than 12 to 14, add 180. Our result is 189.4554, or converted to degrees, minutes and seconds, 189 degrees 27 minutes and 19 seconds. This corresponds to 9 Libra 27 and it is the Ascendant for our example chart. Check it against a computer or table of houses.

Hint: Once you've got this procedure down, list the sequence of buttons to push on your calculator for the Midheaven and Ascendant calculations on a file card. It will be your crib sheet.

E. Calculating the Houses

There are a lot of house systems out there for astrologers to use and not one of them has been proven to the only one worth using. Most people don't even make a choice about what house system they use -- they just follow whatever their teacher used. Their teacher probably did the same. For many years, tables of houses according to the method of Placidus were the only ones readily available, so nearly everyone used them. Abundance does not necessarily make right. Today many astrologers use Koch, a modern system, mostly because certain influential astrologers favor it.

The first house system invented was probably the system called equal houses. In this one, the Midheaven is calculated and the rest of the houses are located at exactly 30 degree intervals. Sounds easy? It is, but they won't let you pass a test with it. Other early house systems acceptable for tests are Alcabitus and Porphyry. Porphyry is interesting because it is logical in its simplicity and is also still very much in use, especially in India. Besides this, it works. In my test of a half-dozen house systems, it held up as well, if not better, than Placidus and Koch. In the Porphyry system, the houses are created by a simple trisection of the arc between the Midheaven and the Ascendant, or any other quadrant. The beauty of the system is that once you've found the cusps of the 11th and 12th, you've got the rest. Here's how you do it.

1. Store the Midheaven (in decimals) in your calculator's memory.

2. Punch in the Ascendant (in decimals) and subtract from it the Midheaven by recalling it from memory.

3. Divide this figure by 3. Write down the result or store it in an extra memory if you have one.

4. Next, add the Midheaven (recall it) to this dividend. The answer is the cusp of the 11th house.

5. Add to the above (11th cusp) the figure from step #3. This is the cusp of the 12th house.

6. The 2nd house is exactly the same degree and minutes as the 12th but two signs ahead in the zodiac. The 3rd house is the same degree and minute as the 11th but four signs ahead. Houses 5, 6, 8, and 9 are exact opposites of houses 11, 12, 2 and 3.

Example: 1. Midheaven = 100.9614
              2. Ascendant (189.4554) - Midheaven = 88.494
              3. 88.494 divided by 3 = 29.498
              4. 29.498 + Midheaven = 130.4594
                   = 11th cusp (10 Leo 27)
              5. 130.4594 + 29.498 = 159.9574
                   = 12th cusp (9 Virgo 57)

6. 2nd house is 9 Scorpio 57, 3rd house is 10 Sagittarius 27. The 5th house is 10 Aquarius 27, the 6th is 9 Pisces 57, the 8th is 9 Taurus 57 and the 9th is 10 Gemini 27. Notice the number symmetry of this system.

Now, with this data, fill out your horoscope wheel and get ready to install the planets.

F. Calculating the Planets' Places

For this step you will need your GMT that you figured way back at the beginning (step A2). You will also need your ephemeris. Basically, you will be figuring out how far each planet traveled in one day (its daily motion) and then finding how far it traveled up to the moment of birth. For the Sun, Moon, and inner planets, use the rules below. You should be able to figure the outer planets in your head.

1. Divide the GMT (in decimals) by 24. Store this figure, called the *Constant Fraction,* in your calculator's memory.

2. Figure the daily motion of the planet in question according to the following formula: Daily Motion = the planet's longitude on the day after the birth (later longitude) minus its longitude on the day of birth (earlier longitude).

3. Multiply the daily motion of the planet by the constant fraction in your calculator's memory.

4. Take the result of step #3 and add it to the planet's longitude on the day of birth (earlier longitude). This equals the planets zodiacal position exactly.

You may come across a few quirks now and then. One is in regard to the two longitude positions being in different signs. For example, suppose the Moon on the day of birth is at 25 degrees of Aries, and on the next day at 10 degrees of Taurus. You add 30 degrees to the latter and subtract the former so it becomes 40 minus 25, or 15 degrees.

Another quirk is in regard to retrogradation. Just do the subtracting in reverse here. If Mercury was at 20 degrees on the day of birth and 18 the next, then figure the difference (2), multiply by the constant fraction and subtract from the day of birth (earlier) longitude.

Example:

1. GMT (5.0166) divided by 24 = 0.2090 (constant fraction)

2a. Daily motion of Sun: Its later longitude, 11 degrees, 21 minutes, 20 seconds, should be expressed in decimals as 11.3555 degrees. Its earlier longitude is 10.3366. Subtract the earlier from the later and we have 0.9989 as the Sun's daily motion.

2b. Daily motion of the Moon: Later longitude is 2 degrees Virgo, 10 minutes and 19 seconds. Converted to decimals this is 2.1744. The earlier longitude is 18 degrees of Leo, 16 minutes and 19 seconds. Converted to decimals, this is 18.2719. Since we can't subtract 18 from 2, we add 30 to the later figure and get the following:
32.1744 - 18.2719 = 13.9025, the Moon's daily motion.

2c. Daily motion of Mercury. Later longitude is 10 degrees and 15.9 minutes of Capricorn. Round this up to 10 Capricorn and 16 minutes and convert to decimals (10.2666). Subtract the earlier longitude of 8 degrees Capricorn 39.8 minutes, rounded up to 8 Capricorn 40 and expressed in decimals (8.6666). The daily motion of Mercury is 1.6.

2d. Do the same for the other planets. From Jupiter on you should be able to do it in your head.

3. Multiply these daily motions by the constant fraction.

Sun: 0.9989 x 0.2090 = 0.2087
Moon: 13.9025 x 0.2090 = 2.9059
Mercury: 1.6 x 0.2090 = 0.3344

4. Add these figures to the earlier longitude to get the true planet's place. Convert decimals back to degrees and minutes for the planets, degrees, minutes and seconds for the Sun and Moon.

Sun .2087 + 10.3366 = 10.54 (10 degrees Cap, 32 min, 43 sec)
Moon 2.9059 + 18.2719 = 21.1778 (21 degrees Leo, 10 min, 40 sec)
Mercury 0.3344 + 8.6666 = 9.0001 (9 Capricorn, exactly)

Put the planets' positions into the chart and you're done with the job. Check it against a computer generated chart and congratulate yourself.

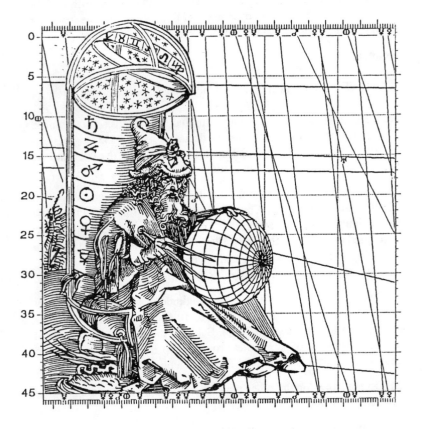

Chart Calculation Resources

Ephemerides:

The American Ephemeris (1901-1930, 1931-80, 1981-90, 1991-2000)
Very complete and accurate. The 1931-1980 volume is clothbound and includes *The American Book of Tables*, described below.

The American Ephemeris for the 20th Century (Midnight)
The whole century in one paperbound volume. Contains all the information that the beginning astrologer would need.

The World Ephemeris for the 20th Century
Another good ephemeris with the essentials. Has larger type.

The Rosicrucian Ephemeris 1900-2000
Also excellent. Unlike older Rosicrucian ephemerides, this one is highly accurate.

Atlases:

The American Atlas
Definitive reference for longitudes, latitudes and time changes in U.S.

The International Atlas
The same for the rest of the world.

House Tables:

The American Book of Tables
Includes Placidus house tables, other useful tables, and detailed instructions on how to cast a chart. All the material in this book is included in *The American Ephemeris and Book of Tables 1931-1980*.

The Koch Book of Tables
Like *The American Book of Tables*, but house tables are Koch system.

Appendix C:
Tables of Planetary Positions

Mercury Stations from 1997 through 2003

#1 station retrograde	*#2 station direct*	*passes #1 station*
12/23/1996 19 Capricorn	1/12/1997 3 Capricorn	2/1/1997
4/15/1997 10 Taurus	5/8/1997 29 Aries	5/25/1997
8/17/1997 16 Virgo	9/9/1997 3 Virgo	9/24/1997
12/7/1997 3 Capricorn	12/27/1997 17 Sagittarius	1/15/1998
3/27/1998 21 Aries	4/20/1998 10 Aries	5/8/1998
7/30/1998 28 Leo	8/23/1998 16 Leo	9/6/1998
11/21/1998 17 Sagittarius	12/11/1998 1 Sagittarius	12/29/1998
3/10/1999 4 Aries	4/2/1999 21 Pisces	4/21/1999
7/12/1999 9 Leo	8/5/1999 29 Cancer	8/20/1999
11/4/1999 2 Sagittarius	11/25/1999 16 Scorpio	12/11/1999
2/21/2000 17 Pisces	3/14/2000 3 Pisces	4/3/2000
6/23/2000 20 Cancer	7/17/2000 10 Cancer	8/1/2000
10/18/2000 16 Scorpio	11/8/2000 0 Scorpio	11/24/2000
2/3/2001 1 Pisces	2/25/2001 15 Aquarius	3/17/2001
6/4/2001 30 Gemini	6/28/2001 21 Gemini	7/12/2001
10/1/2001 30 Libra	10/22/2001 14 Libra	11/7/2001

#1 station retrograde	#2 station direct	passes #1 station
1/18/2002 14 Aquarius	2/8/2002 29 Capricorn	2/28/2002
5/15/2002 10 Gemini	6/8/2002 1 Gemini	6/24/2002
9/14/2002 13 Libra	10/6/2002 28 Virgo	10/21/2002
1/2/2003 28 Capricorn	1/22/2003 12 Capricorn	2/11/2003
4/26/2003 20 Taurus	5/20/2003 11 Taurus	6/5/2003
8/28/2003 26 Virgo	9/20/2003 12 Virgo	10/4/2003

Stationary Periods of Venus 1997 - 2004

#1 station retrograde	#2 station direct	passes #1 station
12/26/1997 4 Aquarius	2/5/1998 18 Capricorn	3/9/1998
7/29/1999 5 Virgo	9/10/1999 19 Leo	10/14/1999
3/8/2001 18 Aries	4/20/2001 1 Aries	5/23/2001
10/10/2002 16 Scorpio	11/21/2002 0 Scorpio	12/22/2002
5/17/2004 26 Gemini	6/29/2004 10 Gemini	8/2/2004

Sign Ingresses of Mars 1997 - 2000

Libra	1/3/1997 (retrogrades back into Virgo)
Scorpio	8/14/1997
Sagittarius	9/28/1997
Capricorn	11/9/1997
Aquarius	12/18/1997
Pisces	1/25/1998
Aries	3/4/1998
Taurus	4/13/1998

Sign Ingresses of Mars (continued)

Gemini	5/24/1998
Cancer	7/6/1998
Leo	8/20/1998
Virgo	10/7/1998
Libra	11/27/1998
Scorpio	1/26/1999 (retrogrades back into Libra)
Sagittarius	9/2/1999
Capricorn	10/17/1999
Aquarius	11/26/1999
Pisces	1/4/2000
Aries	2/12/2000
Taurus	3/23/2000
Gemini	5/3/2000
Cancer	6/16/2000
Leo	8/1/2000
Virgo	9/17/2000
Libra	11/4/2000
Scorpio	12/23/2000

Sign Ingresses of Jupiter 1997 - 2004

Aquarius	1/21/1997
Pisces	2/4/1998
Aries	2/13/1999
Taurus	6/29/1999
Aries	10/23/1999 (retrograde)
Taurus	2/14/2000
Gemini	7/1/2000
Cancer	7/13/2001
Leo	8/1/2002
Virgo	8/27/2003
Libra	9/25/2004

Sign Ingresses of Saturn 1996 - 2003

Aries	4/7/1996
Taurus	6/9/1998
Gemini	8/10/2000
Cancer	6/4/2003

Appendix D:
Astrological Resource Directory

There are many books on astrology available today covering every aspect of the subject. Below are just a few. Many more titles may be found at New Age and Metaphysical Bookshops.

Books about astrology and science:

Gauquelin, Michel. *Birth-Times.* Hill and Wang, 1983. This is only one of several books by Gauquelin that describe his methods of testing astrology. Other titles include *The Cosmic Clocks, The Scientific Basis of Astrology,* and *Planetary Heredity.*

Katzeff, Paul. *Moon Madness.* Robert Hale, 1990. This book looks at social and natural phenomena and correlations with lunar cycles.

Seymour, Percy. *Astrology: The Evidence of Science* Arkana, 1990. The author is an astronomer who has had the courage to actually study astrology and seek reasons for its viability.

Books on the history of astrology:

Tester, S.J. *A History of Western Astrology.* Ballantine Books, 1987. This is a serious, academic study of astrology from ancient times to the Renaissance.

West, Benjamin Anthony. *The Case for Astrology.* Arkana, 1992. In this excellent analysis of astrology's history, West also attacks the scientific objections to the subject and shows them to be full of holes.

Project Hindsight. For information about their translations of ancient astrological texts write: The Golden Hind Press, PO Box 002, Berkeley Springs, WV 25411.

Books on the Symbols of Astrology:

Carter, C.E.O. *Principles of Astrology.* Theosophical Publishing House, Ltd., 1971. A classic primer of astrology from one of England's finest early 20th century astrologers.

Cunningham, Donna. *An Astrological Guide to Self-Awareness.* CRCS Publications, 1978. In this book, Cunningham offers her psychological insights on the symbols of astrology.

Davison, Ronald. *Astrology: The Classic Guide to Understanding Your Horoscope*. Bell, 1963. This book has seen many printings and continues to be a classic on the elements of astrology.

Hand, Robert. *Horoscope Symbols*. Whitford Press, 1981. Every symbol used by practicing astrologers is explained clearly and pragmatically without neglecting the psychological and spiritual dimensions.

Lewi, Grant. *Astrology for the Millions*. Llewellyn Publications, 1964. An old favorite from a great American astrologer.

Mayo, Jeff. *The Planets and Human Behavior*. L.N. Fowler, 1972, and *Teach Yourself Astrology*. Shambala Publications, 1964. Both titles offer readers an unusually clear and rational view of astrology's multi-level perspective on the human condition.

McEvers, Joan, ed. *Planets: The Astrological Tools*. Llewellyn, 1989. This is one of the Llewellyn New World series books on astrology. Each volume has a central theme that is discussed by several astrologers, presenting their own unique perspectives on the topic. The volumes on the basics, ie. houses, signs, etc. are highly recommended.)

Rodgers-Gallagher, Kim. *Astrology for the Light Side of the Brain*. ACS, 1994. This hilarious book covers nearly all sides of astrology. It's a little like the book you're reading now, but funnier.

Rudhyar, Dane. *The Astrological Houses,* Doubleday, 1972, and *Astrological Signs*, Shambala, 1963. Rudhyar's writings on the houses and the signs have influenced several generations of astrologers.

Dictionaries of astrology:

The Arkana Dictionary of Astrology. Arkana, 1985.
The Larousse Encyclopedia of Astrology.
DeVore, Nicholas. *Encyclopedia of Astrology*. Philosophical Library.

Books on Psychological astrology:

Forrest, Steven. *The Inner Sky*. ACS, 1985. In this and other books, *The Changing Sky* and *The Night Speaks,* Forrest writes passionately and philosophically on how astrology encourages free-will and choice.

Greene, Liz and Howard Sasportas. *The Development of the Personality*. Samuel Weiser, 1987, and *The Dynamics of the Unconscious*. Samuel Wiser, 1988. These two books are transcriptions of seminars on psychological astrology presented by two masters.

Rudhyar, Dane. *The Astrology of Personality.* Doubleday, 1936, 1970. This is the first of many books Rudhyar wrote on astrology. In it he approaches astrology from a philosophical, psychological, and spiritual perspective.

Relationships:

Davison, Ronald. *Synastry.* Aurora Press, 1983. A guidebook to traditional chart comparisons, planet by planet.

Hand, Robert. *Planets in Composite.* Para Research, 1975. A guide to the meanings of the planets in a chart derived from two birthcharts.

Idemon, Richard. *Through the Looking Glass.* Samuel Weiser, 1992. This astro-psychology book approaches relationships as reflections of our inner selves.

Practical uses of astrology:

Cozzi, Steve. *Planets in Locality.* St. Paul, MN: Llewellyn Publications. 1988. A guide to the astrological influences of your location. Includes astro-mapping, local space astrology, principles of Feng Shui.

Hathaway, Edith. *Navigating by the Stars.* Llewellyn Publications, 1991. This book contains well-organized technical information on many uses of astrology, including locational and electional astrology.

Scofield, Bruce. *The Timing of Events: Electional Astrology.* Astrolabe, 1984. A technical overview of traditional electional astrology. Includes many examples.

Transits and forecasting:

Hand, Robert. *Planets in Transit.* Whitford Press, 1976. An excellent astrological "cookbook" for interpreting transits.

Negus, Joan. *Astro-Alchemy: Making the Most of your Transits.* ACS, 1989. A good, down-to-earth approach to working with transits to your natal chart.

Astrology and Computers:

Foreman, Patricia. *Computers and Astrology.* Good Earth Publications, Box 160, Columbus, NC 28722. This is a 320-page book that contains much useful information about astrology and computers. It includes a large dictionary of astrology and has many useful tables.

Useful and Informative Periodicals

American Astrology. 475 Park Ave. S., New York, NY 10016. An excellent monthly magazine with a long tradition of publishing insightful and intelligent (some technical) articles on astrology.

Dell Horoscope. P.O. Box 53352, Boulder, CO 80332. Long been a leader in the large-scale publishing of intelligent articles on astrology.

Horoscope Guide. PO Box 226, Ft. Washington, PA 19034. Publishes mostly entry-level articles and forecasts on astrology.

Llewellyn's Astrological Calendar, Llewellyn's Moon Sign Book, Llewellyn's Sun Sign Book. Published annually by Llewellyn Publications, P.O. Box 64383-451, St. Paul, MN 55164. These are three annuals which offer useful astrological information about the year ahead, excellent articles by leading astrologers, and much more.

The Mercury Hour. 3509 Waterlick Road C-7, Lynchburg, VA 24502. This quarterly magazine is a format for discussions within the astrological community.

The Mountain Astrologer P.O.Box 970, Cedar Ridge, CA 95924-0970. America's best astrology magazine. It has great articles on current topics, theme issues, columns, humor, reviews, and more.

Welcome to Planet Earth. P.O. Box 5164, Eugene, OR 97405. This monthly magazine offers interesting astrological insights into current events and happenings worldwide.

Valliere, James T. *Valliere's Natural Cycles Almanac.* Published annually. Available from Astrolabe, P.O. Box 1750, Brewster, MA 02631. This graphic almanac offers monthly graphs of planetary rises, culminations, sets, and lower culminations. Great for doing electional astrology and for diurnal charts.

Sources for Astrological Software

AIR Software, 115 Caya Avenue, West Hartford, CT 06110. (800) 659-1247. AIR offers a wide variety of unique programs, many based on the work, research, and creative ideas of professional astrologer Alphee Lavoie.

Andromeda Software, P.O. Box 605, Amherst NY 14226-0605. Reliable vendor providing astronomy shareware for IBMs and compatibles.

Astro Communications Services, Inc. PO Box 34487, San Diego, CA 92163-4487. Info (619) 492-9919, Orders (800) 888-9983. Although this company is best known for outstanding chart service and publications, they also sell astrological software -- their own and software from other companies.

Astro-Cybernetics, MMA PO Box 250012, W. Bloomfield, MI 48325. (800) 662-3349. Produces the versatile Pathfinder software.

Astrolabe Software, P.O. Box 1750, 350 Underpass Road, Brewster, MA 02631. Info (508) 896-9567. Orders (800) 843-6682. A pioneer in software for astrologers and has a reputation for bug-free programs. They offer a very complete line of software and tools for astrology.

Cosmic Patterns, P.O. Box 140790, Gainesville, FL, 32614. (352) 373-1504. Produces the versatile Kepler Program.

Halloran Software, PO Box 75713, Los Angeles, CA 90075. (800)-SEA-GOAT. This company offers quality programs at low prices.

Matrix Software, 315 Marion Avenue, Big Rapids, MI 49307. (616) 796-2483. Orders (800) PLANETS. A pioneer in the field of astrological software, Matrix offers a wide variety of programs known for their versatility and excellent graphics.

Microcycles, P.O. Box 3175, Culver City, CA 90231. (800) 829-2537. This distributor of astrological software carries every program on astrology that is available and offers advice and support. Prices are the same as the manufacturer. In addition, Microcycles also carries numerology, tarot, I-Ching, and other divinatory software.

Time Cycles Research, 375 Willetts Ave., Waterford, CT 06385. (800) 827-2240. Offers the Io Series, a line of software for Apple Mac.

Zephyr Services, 1900 Murray Ave., Pittsburgh, PA 15217. (800) 533-6666. Along with a few astrology programs, this company offers a selection of novel astronomy programs.

National Astrological Organizations

American Federation of Astrologers. P.O. Box 22040, Tempe, AZ 85282. AFA holds a major convention every two years.

Association for Astrological Networking (AFAN). 8306 Wilshire Blvd., Suite 537, Beverly Hills, CA 90211. Focus is on the legality of astrology and the support of the astrological community in general.

Fraternity for Canadian Astrologers (FCA). 91 Bowmore Rd., Toronto, M4L 3J1 Canada. Publishes a journal and holds conferences.

International Society for Astrological Research (ISAR). P.O. Box 38613, Los Angeles, CA 90038. One of the larger astrological organizations in the U.S., part of the United Astrology Congress (UAC).

National Council for Geocosmic Research (NCGR). PO Box 501078, Malabar, FL 32950-1078. A large, national organization with local chapters throughout the U.S.A. Write for a listing of local chapters.

Astrological Certifications and Educational Programs

American Federation of Astrologers (AFA)
PO Box 22040, Tempe, AZ 85285-2040
(Offers professional certification with the passing of full-day exam.)

Aquarius Workshops
PO Box 260556, Encino, CA 91426

Astrology Institute
17 Locke Lane
Lexington MA 02173

The Church of Light, 2341 Coral Street, Los Angeles, CA 90031-2916

City of Atlanta, Georgia (This city requires practicing astrologers to pass an examination on astrology in order to be licensed.)

Faculty of Astrological Studies
Box 7470, London WC1N 3XX England

International Society for Astrological Research, Inc. (ISAR)
PO Box 38613, Los Angeles, CA 90036-0613

Jeff Mayo School of Astrology c/o L.N. Fowler & Co. Ltd.
1201/3 High Road, Romford, Essex RM6 4DH Great Britain

National Council for Geocosmic Research, Inc. (NCGR)
PO Box 501078, Malabar, FL 32950-1078
(NCGR offers astrological proficiency exams on 4 levels)

Astrological Chart Calculation Services

Astro*Carto*Graphy
Astro Numeric Service
Box 336-BI
Ashland, OR 97520

Astro Communications Services, Inc.
PO Box 34487
San Diego, CA 92163-4487

Astrolabe
PO Box 1750
Brewster, MA 02631

Astrological Bureau of Ideas
PO Box 251
Wethersfield, CT 06109

Charts Unlimited
F2 Stonehedge Drive
South Burlington, VT 05403

Directories of Practicing Astrologers

International Directory of Astrologers
ARC Directory
2920 E. Monte Vista
Tucson, AZ 85716

NCGR Directory of Professional Astrologers
NCGR
PO Box 1220
Dunkirk, MD 20754-9998

Also Available from
One Reed Publications

Day-Signs: Native American Astrology From Ancient Mexico,
**by Bruce Scofield. 1991, ISBN 0-9628031-0-3, 220 pages,
paperback, $11.95.**

This book contains the first practical delineations ever published for
the 20 day-signs used in Maya and Aztec astrology. Like the Western
12-sign zodiac, the 20 day-signs describe personality, temperament,
talents, and challenges. In addition, this book contains a 50-page
introduction to the day-signs and 30 pages of tables that allow readers
to easily determine individual day-signs for the 20th century.

Signs of Time: An Introduction to Mesoamerican Astrology,
**by Bruce Scofield. 1993, ISBN 0-9628031-1-1, 220 pages,
paperback, $11.95.**

The entire spectrum of Mesoamerican astrology is presented in this
unique companion volume to *Day-Signs.* Included is the 260-day
Tzolkin, the 9 Lords of the Night, the Long Count (Mayan Calendar),
the cycle of the Katuns, and the 8-year cycle of Venus. The material is
first presented directly, then suggestions about how it might be applied
are offered in a separate section of the book.

Persephone is Transpluto, **by Valerie Vaughan.
1995, ISBN 0-9628031-2-X, 256 pages, paperback, $12.95.**

This book is a pioneering and scholarly investigation into the mythology, astrology, and scientific discovery of the planet beyond Pluto.
Astronomers have long suspected the existence of a planet beyond
Pluto (Planet X) and have computed tentative orbital parameters.
Valerie Vaughan sets out the possible astrological meaning of this
"undiscovered" planet based on the myth of Persephone. To support
her powerful arguments, Vaughan marshals evidence from astronomy,
astrology, archaeology, ancient history, mythology, and even UFOlogy.

The above books may be ordered from:
One Reed Publications, PO Box 561, Amherst, MA 01004-0561.
*Please enclose $1.50 P&H for one book,
plus $.50 for each additional book.*